MW00609780

PIERRE HERMÉ

MACARONS

Photography Bernhard Winkelmann

Grub Street • London

CONTENTS

96   ## Signature Macarons

'My macarons composed over the years and my preferences which have become my signatures.'

156 Made-to-order Macarons

'I designed some "haute-couture" macarons for and with specific clients.'

178 Exceptions

'Innovations and interpretations based on exceptional ingredients.'

203 Useful Addresses

207 Acknowledgements

© Jean-Louis Bloch-Lainé

THE MAN WHO HEARS RECIPES IN HIS HEAD

By Clémence Boulouque

PIERRE HERMÉ, YOU GREW UP IN A FAMILY OF PASTRY CHEFS. YOU WERE APPRENTICED TO GASTON LENÔTRE. WHERE DOES YOUR PASSION FOR MACARONS COME FROM?

When I learnt how to make macarons in 1976, pastry chefs were still confined to a very limited repertoire: coffee, chocolate, raspberry, and vanilla macarons – minus the vanilla cream – were just two shells stuck together. So, I started to wonder what gave macarons their flavour: the shell, of course, but it's mostly the filling. That's what I wanted to work on, and it's still my priority today. Apart from the diversity of flavours, what makes my macarons unique is that I fill them more generously than other people. You don't necessarily notice that sort of detail but it makes a real difference to the flavour. Then, when I was at Fauchon, I expanded the range, with pistachio, lemon and rose. These days, I list those under Classics, but back then, they were really adventurous. In 1994, I began to see how I could use the macaron to experiment and innovate. And that's how lime and basil, hazelnut and white truffle, and olive oil and vanilla came about. Then, I combined a flavour with contrasting textures, especially by adding elements. For example, in the olive oil macaron, I add tiny pieces of olive so that the flavour is released a little at a time and not uniformly as it would be if you blended it into the cream. In 2003, I saw the macaron as a kind of link, and I applied my research and findings from other cakes, like

a scientist conducting experiments. Then in 2004-2005, with the *Past-Future Collection* [*Rétrospective-Perspective*], I worked laterally, as though I could transpose flavours from one cake to another.

YOU PRODUCE 'COLLECTIONS' LIKE A FASHION DESIGNER. YOU OFTEN GIVE YOUR CREATIONS POETIC NAMES. DO YOU LOOK FOR INSPIRATION OUTSIDE THE TRADITIONAL TERRITORIES OF THE PASTRY CHEF?

It's often unconscious. I admire the American artist Sol LeWitt and Yves Klein's use of colour and materials. I'm fascinated by certain artists, like Jean-Michel Duriez or Patou's 'nose'. What we do is similar: inventing a perfume and bringing it to fruition is like imagining a flavour. Finding a name is almost the hardest part, and I refuse to use English names. I came up with the name 'Ispahan' while I was there. I was looking for a name that would evoke the rose petals used in the recipe and I thought it would be a poetic reference. I had the gardens of Ispahan in my mind. But basically, my work is a kind of architecture of taste and sensations, and my main aim is the pleasure of the person who tastes it.

Japan is one source of inspiration among others. I extended my range of flavour combinations with wasabi and candied grapefruit for the contrast. But you're right, my work produces hybrids, on different levels and throughout my work in general. For example, I've just created an Ispahan croissant which I tried to make taste like the cake, while at the same time working on the jellification process to give the raspberry jelly the true flavour of the fruit.

In any profession, you have to know the customs and practices, the materials and history and your predecessors. You can forget about all that in the short term, but if you want to exist in the long term, you're going to need that knowledge. I don't believe in spontaneous creation and moments of enlightenment. Am I an iconoclast? Knowing my profession in detail and appreciating its bases has helped me to 'transgress' in the full knowledge of what I'm doing. I've also been helped and encouraged by my friend and associate, Charles Znaty; he was the one who made me work on the macaron, make it fashionable and push my experiments and ideas further. To give you an example: pairing chocolate with the macaron. Recently, I created a chocolate macaron sweet decorated with a tiny macaron, but I felt I hadn't reached the limits of my research. My experiments always end with the question: is it interesting or is it good? If I can only answer 'yes' to the first question, I put the project aside. It's something I can think about for 30 seconds or for four years. I spent ages trying to adapt the flavour of Moroccan carrot and orange salad. It took me a year or two to bring it to fruition and raise the carrot to something other than just a vegetable without losing its flavour.

There are two stages to each of my recipes: the point of creation, and the moment it becomes a recipe which chefs at Pierre Hermé can follow. The ability to communicate is just as much a part of the work of creation, even if it's less visible. The artist Sol LeWitt worked in a similar way: he used to get other people to make what he had envisaged. He was able to describe his work. I should have liked to meet him, but sadly, he died in 2007 and it never happened. For the book, I got our ten-year-old daughter, Sarah, to make macarons. I guided her using the book's instructions, and the macarons she made were wonderful and very tasty. 'It was great work making my chocolate macarons!' she said. 'I loved making them, because with you it was easy.' They weren't quite as round as the ones in the photos, of course, but the texture was the same. There's no secret to it: all you have to do is follow the steps, get to know the recipe and **tame** it. The real problem would be if you said the recipe hadn't worked out when you hadn't really followed the process to the letter. And that's essential. You can't start baking before you have the recipe to hand, because, crucially, I never miss out a stage – which is why the recipes might seem rather long – but it seemed essential to me to describe every detail of the different steps. The book is also an index of creation and is divided into chapters that organize the macarons according to *Classics, Fetish Flavours, Signature Macarons, Made-to-Order Macarons* and finally *Exceptions* devised at the request of specific clients. The *Exceptions* are the most complicated to make, but again, I guide the reader through the process one step at a time.

Portrait in a macaron: it is perhaps in this little round delicacy that Pierre Hermé and his innovation are best reflected and encapsulated. Pierre Hermé is a pioneer who pays tribute to the pastry-chef tradition he would never and could never leave. An autodidact who quotes the artist Sol LeWitt, he hears recipes in his head.

'He can jot down a recipe from scratch on a scrap of paper, and if you follow it, you get exactly the result he described,' says Charles Znaty, Pierre Hermé's esteemed associate and friend. Like a composer, 'he's produced harmonies you'd never have thought of, like banana and avocado. Or he pairs a macaron with foie gras. His work is exotic but never about exile,' adds Ingrid Astier, whose erudite cookbooks demonstrate as much knowledge of Cioran as they do of the art of chocolate. 'Even when he seems to go off-course, you always end up on the right note. That's real harmony for you.' 'He comes up with outrageous associations, like chocolate and foie gras,' continues Hélène Darrouze, a female chef. But although she dubs him her 'big brother', his colleague is keen to stress that he works on his own and seldom seeks advice upwards before producing his creations.

It is now over 15 years since Pierre Hermé acted on the advice and intuition of his associate to give the macaron its own life. That was before the fashion he created really took off. Nowadays, macarons seem to be everywhere, but Pierre Hermé is apparently unaffected by the craze and pursues his research and his logical, often lonely way, as he ventures into new-found lands of flavour.

Ingrid Astier describes the macaron as a swashbuckling adventurer: 'I love its rebellious side. It's a rebel that's fallen out with all the other *petits fours* to forge its own life among its own people on a totally different planet. That's what makes it a winner and eminently loveable: it's rebellious but Protean at the same time.'

Julie Andrieu, the author of a dozen cookbooks, uses the same word 'rebellious', in her *Confidences sucrées* (*Sweet Secrets*), which she wrote with Pierre Hermé: 'There can be something consensual about baking but he's gone beyond that. He's a bit of a rebel without being provocative. You get a sense of progress and arrival. Without realising, he has raised the art of the pastry chef to an intellectual level and made it poetic. He works on what his clients feel. You get the sense you're learning something, especially about flavour combinations, like green tea and chestnut. Gluttony is seen as a deadly sin (though only because of a mistranslation), but he promotes the pleasure of gluttony and makes it something dignified and refined. That's how you make waves in gastronomy.'

The macaron reveals the pastry chef's literary side. Following his inspirations and innovations, forming preferences, comparing, and even growing excited, is like admiring an author and waiting for his next book to come out. Quite simply, you get hooked: 'There's something very endearing about the macaron,' puts in Ingrid Astier, 'and an obvious link with collections of colour crayons. You want all the colours in the box. Yes, the macaron is a *petit four* to take to your heart. And you know there's always love involved when you give someone macarons. It's what remains of the child in the adult.' But there's nothing retrograde about letting the child in us nurture the adult, quite the opposite in fact, for childhood is a realm that is protected from adults. Pierre Hermé's macarons are not just virtuoso performances: the new recipes are also about hesitant hands that might play a wrong note, and taming them is about retrieving some of the hesitancy of childhood. Pierre Hermé is a teacher and a maestro. Pierre, reflected in his macarons, is a pioneer in tireless pursuit of adult alchemy for emotions that will recapture childhood.

PIERRE HERMÉ'S MACARON SECRETS REVEALED

I SELECT MY OWN ALMONDS. My favourites are Valencia Spanish almonds, and I grind them myself, because that way, I can both control where they come from and obtain the ideal consistency.

TO MAKE THE MACARON BATTER, I use exclusively what I describe as 'liquefied' egg whites. Why 'liquefied'? Because the egg whites will liquefy if you sit them in the fridge for several days, preferably a week. During that time, the egg whites lose their elasticity, the albumen breaks down and they will be much easier to whisk to soft peaks without the risk of turning 'grainy'. And you don't have to worry about bacteria because they will be cooked in the oven at a high temperature.

SEVERAL OF THE FRUIT FILLINGS I MAKE involve white chocolate, which has splendid flavour-carrying properties. It has the advantage of receding into the background and bringing out the taste of ingredients that are added to it.

I FILL THE MACARON SHELLS VERY GENEROUSLY with ganache or cream, because it's above all the filling that gives the macarons their flavour. When they are baked and assembled, the 24-hour standing time in the fridge is essential. During that time, the ambient humidity and the moisture of the filling have time to flavour the shells slightly and improve the texture. Next day, they will have the perfect consistency of a macaron just the way I like them, a little bit crisp but soft and fondant for a moment of pure delight.

TO ENJOY THEM AT ROOM TEMPERATURE, take the macarons out of the fridge two hours before serving. Macarons should not be eaten the day they are made, because they will be too dry. They need the ageing time described above.

THIRTY-TWO STEPS TO SUCCESSFUL MACARON SHELLS

To make Pierre Hermé's macarons, simply follow the instructions one step at a time.

On your work surface, lay out all the ingredients in the recipe for the macaron you have chosen to make.

1. WEIGH OUT THE EGG WHITES indicated in each recipe described as 'liquefied' egg whites. Separate the whites from the yolks. Weigh out the necessary quantity of egg whites into two bowls.

2. COVER THE BOWLS WITH CLINGFILM. Using the point of a sharp knife, pierce the film with holes. It is best to prepare the egg whites several days in advance, preferably a week, so that they lose their elasticity. Set the bowls aside in the fridge.

3. ON THE DAY YOU BAKE THE MACARONS, prepare two piping bags. Disposable plastic piping bags are best. The first is for the batter, the second is for the ganache or cream filling. Using kitchen scissors, cut the points off the piping bags 5 cm from the end.

4. INSERT A NOZZLE (plain No 11) right to the end of the bag.

5. TO MAKE SURE THE MACARON BATTER doesn't escape when you spoon it into the bag, push the nozzle firmly into the bag with your finger.

6. PREPARE THE BAKING TRAYS for the shells. Lay the template of circles on the first baking tray, then cover it with a sheet of baking parchment. (To make your own template of circles, see page 35) Depending on their size, you will need three or four baking trays.

7. FOR THE MACARON BATTER. Weigh out the ground almonds and the icing sugar separately.

8. IN A BOWL, stir together the ground almonds and icing sugar. Place a medium-mesh sieve over a large bowl. Sift by gently shaking the sieve.

9. IF YOU HAVE CHOSEN A RECIPE that includes food colouring(s), mix it/them into the first bowl of egg whites.

10. POUR THE COLOURED (OR NOT) EGG WHITES into the bowl of ground almonds and icing sugar, but do not stir.

11. ON THE SCALES, weigh out the caster sugar and water in two separate bowls.

12. POUR THE WATER INTO A SMALL SAUCEPAN THEN ADD THE SUGAR. Put the probe of an electronic thermometer into the sugar. Cook over a medium heat and as soon as the sugar reaches 115°C, simultaneously start to whisk the second quantity of liquefied egg whites to soft peaks at high speed in an electric mixer with a whisk attachment. Dip a pastry brush in cold water. When the sugar boils, clean the sides with the damp brush.

13. WHEN THE SUGAR REACHES 118°C, take the saucepan straight off the heat. Pour the hot sugar over the egg whites before the meringue is fully formed. Continue whisking at high speed for another minute.

14. REDUCE THE WHISKING SPEED to a medium speed and continue whisking the egg whites for about two minutes. You have just made an Italian meringue.

15. WAIT UNTIL THE ITALIAN MERINGUE has cooled down to 50°C by the electronic thermometer (about four or five minutes) before taking it out of the bowl of the electric mixer.

16. TIP THE ITALIAN MERINGUE out of the mixer bowl. Using the spatula, stir it into the mixture of icing sugar and ground almonds folding in the batter and stirring outwards from the middle to the sides, rotating the bowl in your hands as you stir.

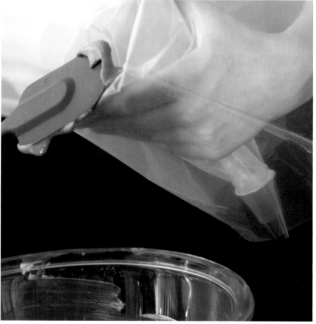

17. CONTINUE STIRRING, still from the middle of the batter out to the sides of the bowl and rotating the bowl as you do. When the batter is just starting to turn glossy, it is ready. The batter should resemble slightly runny cake dough.

18. TAKE THE FIRST PIPING BAG you prepared in your half-open hand. Scoop up a little batter on the spatula. Scrape it into the bag. Fill the bag with half the batter by scraping it on to the side of the bag.

19. SQUEEZE THE BATTER into the bag so that it slips right down to the end of the piping bag. This is important because there should not be any space or air bubbles in the batter.

20. TWIST THE END OF THE BAG down tightly with several twists to trap the batter firmly in the bag.

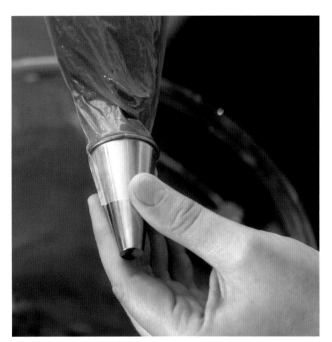

21. PULL ON THE NOZZLE to begin piping the shells.

22. POSITION YOURSELF ABOUT 2 CM above the first baking tray. Hold the piping bag vertically and gently squeeze the top to pipe out the first shell which should be just short of 3.5 cm in diameter, as the batter will spread during cooking.

23. STOP SQUEEZING THE PIPING BAG. Move forwards a little and give a quarter turn to block the batter. Continue piping the shells leaving a 2 cm gap between them and arranging them in staggered rows. This is why the template is very important.

24. WHEN YOU HAVE USED UP ALL THE BATTER in the bag, fill it up again with the other half of the batter. Continue piping the shells on to the other baking trays (with the template).

25. TO FLATTEN OUT THE POINTS that have formed on the shells, lift up the baking trays one by one and rap them lightly on the work surface covered with a kitchen towel.

26. LIFT A CORNER of the baking parchment, slide out the template and lay it on the other baking trays, one by one as you use them.

27. TO MAKE SURE the baking parchment doesn't move during cooking time in the fan oven, stick down the four corners with dabs of the batter. Press gently on the corners to make sure they are firmly held in place.

28. ALLOW THE SHELLS TO STAND at room temperature for about 30 minutes until a skin forms on the surface. The batter should not stick to your finger.

29. PRE-HEAT THE FAN OVEN to 180°C, but be aware that the cooking temperature in your oven may vary between 165°C and 190°C. The shells should not change colour during cooking. You should set the temperature of your oven according to the type of oven you have.

30. DEPENDING ON THE SIZE OF YOUR OVEN, you can put all three or four baking trays in the oven together, otherwise, bake them in two batches. Bake for 12 minutes, briefly opening and shutting the oven door twice to let out the steam. Open the door the first time after eight minutes (at that point the 'foot' of the shells will be cooked) then a second time after 10 minutes.

31. AS SOON AS YOU TAKE the macaron shells out of the oven, slide the baking parchment on to the work surface. This is important: if you leave the shells on the baking tray, they will go on cooking. Allow the shells to cool on the baking parchment.

32. CAREFULLY UNSTICK half the cooled shells from the baking parchment, one at a time by hand. Lay them flat-side up, side by side on another sheet of baking parchment. They are ready to be filled. You can also store them for 48 hours in the fridge or freeze them.

NINE STEPS TO A SUCCESSFUL CHOCOLATE GANACHE

Whatever kind of ganache or cream you use in the macarons, the process is the same. It is essential to pour the hot liquid over the mixture in thirds and to start stirring for a few minutes in the centre of the bowl before working your way out towards the sides of the bowl in widening concentric circles.

1. USING A SERRATED KNIFE, chop up the chocolate into very small pieces on a chopping board placed on a kitchen cloth to hold it still. To do this, hold the blade of the knife in one hand, lay the palm of your other hand flat on the blade and make a rocking movement up and down.

2. TIP THE CHOPPED CHOCOLATE into a heat-resistant bowl. Pour hot water into a saucepan of smaller dimensions than the bowl: the bowl should not touch the bottom of the pan. Put the bowl of chocolate in the saucepan and place over a low heat.

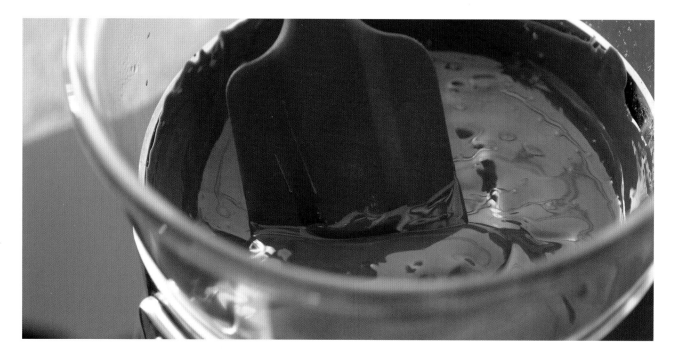

3. AT NO TIME SHOULD YOU LET THE WATER IN THE SAUCEPAN BOIL; it should be barely simmering. When the chocolate starts to melt, stir it gently with a spatula. The chunks of chocolate should melt in two or three minutes. Remove the bowl from the saucepan as soon as the chocolate has melted and stir it to a smooth consistency.

4. IN A SMALL SAUCEPAN, bring the cream to the boil, stirring with a whisk to prevent the cream sticking to the base of the pan.

5. POUR A THIRD OF THE HOT CREAM into the centre of the bowl and start whisking for a few minutes. Don't worry if the cream separates when you pour in the hot cream. This is caused by molecules of fat in the cream and chocolate separating.

6. POUR THE SECOND THIRD of the hot cream into the centre of the bowl. Stir the centre until the consistency starts to thicken. Work your way out to the sides of the bowl in widening circles.

7. POUR THE LAST THIRD of the hot cream into the centre and work your way out to the sides of the bowl in widening circles.

8. POUR THE GANACHE into a gratin dish measuring about 22-24 cm in length. Scrape out the bowl with the spatula.

9. COVER THE GANACHE with clingfilm so that the film is touching the surface. Allow the ganache to cool before putting it in the fridge until it thickens.

EIGHT STEPS TO ASSEMBLING THE MACARONS

1. TAKE A SECOND PIPING BAG in your half-open hand. Using the spatula, scoop up a small amount of ganache or cream. Scrape it into the bag. Squeeze the ganache (or cream) into the bag so that it slips right down to the end of the piping bag.

2. TWIST THE END OF THE BAG down tightly with several twists to trap the ganache (or cream) firmly in the bag.

3. PULL THE NOZZLE to begin piping the ganache or cream on to the shells.

4. POSITION YOURSELF ABOUT 2 CM above the first baking tray. Hold the piping bag vertically and squeeze it very gently. Pipe a generous mound of ganache on to each shell, making sure you leave an edge of about 3 mm.

5. UNSTICK THE SECOND BATCH OF SHELLS FROM THE BAKING PARCHMENT. Cover each filled shell with a second shell and press down very lightly.

6. IF THE MACARONS CONTAIN A SQUARE OF JELLY or ganache, pipe a little less ganache on to the shells. Press lightly on the centre of the square.

7. PIPE A DOT OF GANACHE or cream on to the square. Top each one with a second shell and press down lightly.

8. PLACE THE FILLED MACARONS SIDE BY SIDE ON BAKING TRAYS or on trays covered with baking parchment. Put them in the fridge for 24 hours before serving. Take them back out two hours before serving to be enjoyed at the ideal temperature.

UTENSILS

DISPOSABLE PLASTIC PIPING BAGS WITH NOZZLES. Kitchen scissors to cut the ends off the bags. The nozzles to form the shells should be 11 to 12 mm.

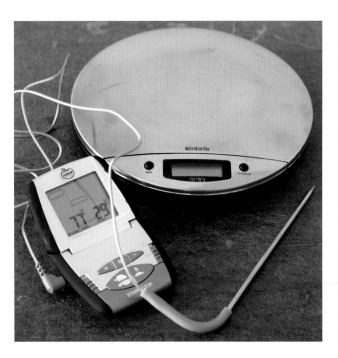

AN ELECTRONIC THERMOMETER is essential to take all the temperatures. Accurate scales to the nearest gram.

THICK GLASS BOWLS with a rounded base (they can also be stainless steel) in different sizes.

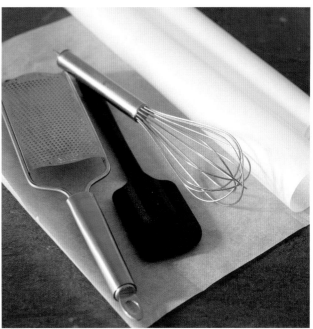

A MEDIUM-MESH SIEVE to sift the ground almonds and icing sugar. Three or four baking trays so that you can bake all the macaron shells in a single batch.

A MICROPLANE GRATER to obtain the finest possible zests for the fruit jellies. A flexible rubber spatula to stir the batter or scrape out the bowls. It should be very flexible and ideally withstand temperatures up to 300°C. A hand whisk. Baking parchment.

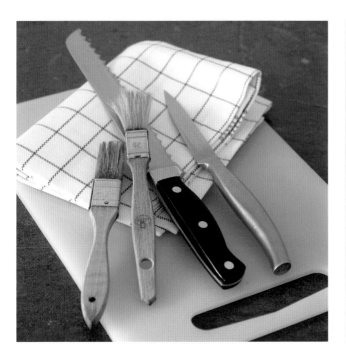

PASTRY BRUSHES. A serrated knife to chop up the chocolate (Kitchen Aid). Kitchen knife (Zwilling).

A GRATIN DISH measuring about 22-24 cm in length for chilling the ganache or cream and for the jellies (which you will then cut into squares of jelly or ganache). Transparent clingfilm.

FREQUENTLY ASKED QUESTIONS

THE TEMPLATE FOR THE MACARON SHELLS

To make it easier to form the macaron shells, you can make your own template.

Cut a sheet of baking parchment so that it fits inside the baking tray. Draw circles using a glass, small cup or a plain round pastry cutter measuring 3.5 cm in diameter. Stagger the lines and space the circles 2 cm apart.

OVER-COOKED OR DRY SHELLS?

Spray them lightly with water.

WHAT TO DO IF THE GANACHE IS TOO COMPACT WHEN IT COOLS

You can bring it back to a flexible consistency by melting it gently in a bowl placed over a saucepan of barely simmering water or in a microwave, stirring it as little as possible so as not to incorporate too much air.

IMPORTANT TO KNOW FOR THE JELLY, GANACHE, CREAM OR COMPOTE SQUARES IN THE MACARONS

Line the base and sides of a wide gratin dish with clingfilm so that it overlaps the edges; this will make it easier to turn the mixture out of the dish. Tip the mixture into the dish to a depth of no more than 4 mm, otherwise the squares will be too high and you will have trouble topping the macarons with a second shell.

Chill the mixture for 1 hour in the fridge then put the dish in the freezer. Take hold of the clingfilm. Turn the tray over on to a work surface. Cut the slab into squares then put the squares back in the dish and return the dish to the freezer until you are ready to use them in the macarons. They will defrost during the 24 hours' standing time in the fridge. This will provide the necessary moisture for soft macarons.

If some of the mixture is left over, tip it into another container and enjoy!

WHAT IS CHOCOLATE COUVERTURE?

This is a professional term for chocolate, whether milk, dark or ivory white. Chocolate couverture is sold in blocks 2 cm thick or more, which is why you need to use a serrated knife to chop it up into tiny pieces.

WHAT IS THE TITANIUM OXIDE POWDER FOR?

To blanch the macarons. The 'plain' batter is a beige colour. The powder has no smell or taste and it will not affect the flavour of the macaron.

MELTING THE CHOPPED CHOCOLATE IN THE MICROWAVE

Tip the chopped chocolate into a container, which should not be glass or metal. Set the oven to a medium power not above 600 Watts, then heat in intervals of no more than 10 to 15 seconds, stirring gently after each interval. The chocolate should take a minute to melt.

FOOD COLOURING

The colourings are added to make your macarons glisten enticingly. Use them sparingly. In all my recipes, I suggest the ideal quantities and combinations. To help you, I have selected several suppliers (see page 205)

THE CLASSICS

'OVER THE YEARS, NEW CLASSICS HAVE BEEN ADDED TO THE TIME-HONOURED
CLASSIC FLAVOURS.'

BITTER CHOCOLATE MACARON

FOR A LONG FINISH ON THE TONGUE, I USE MAXIMUM STRENGTH CHOCOLATE AND ADD CACAO PÂTE UNSWEETENED WITH 100% COCOA SOLIDS) OR 100% DARK CHOCOLATE, WHICH YOU CAN BUY FROM SOME ARTISANAL BAKERS.

Makes about 72 macarons (or about 144 shells)

PREPARATION TIME:

about 1 hour

COOKING TIME:

about 25 minutes

STANDING TIME:

30 minutes

REFRIGERATION:

2 hours + 24 hours

FOR THE MACARON SHELLS

120g cacao pâte (or dark chocolate 100% cocoa)

300g ground almonds

300g icing sugar

110g 'liquefied' egg whites (see page 11)

4.5g carmine red food colouring (or cochineal)

+

300g caster sugar

75g mineral water

110g 'liquefied' egg whites (see page 11)

FOR THE BITTER CHOCOLATE GANACHE

400g liquid crème fraîche or whipping cream (35% fat)

360g Valrhona Guanaja couverture chocolate

40g cacao pâte (or dark chocolate, 100% cocoa solids)

140g 'La Viette' butter (sweet butter from Charentes) at room temperature

TO FINISH

Cocoa powder

Sift together the icing sugar and ground almonds. Chop up the cacao pâte and melt it at 50°C in a bowl over a pan of barely simmering water. Stir the food colouring into the first portion of liquefied egg whites and add this to the bowl of icing sugar and ground almonds but do not stir.

Bring the water and sugar to boil at 118°C. When the syrup reaches 115°C, simultaneously start whisking the second portion of liquefied egg whites to soft peaks.

When the sugar reaches 118°C, pour it over the egg whites. Whisk and allow the meringue to cool down to 50°C, then add it to the bowl of icing sugar and ground almonds, stir, then fold in the melted cacao. Spoon the batter into a piping bag fitted with a plain nozzle.

Pipe rounds of the batter measuring about 3.5 cm in diameter, 2 cm apart on baking trays lined with baking parchment. Using a sieve, sprinkle them with a light dusting of cocoa powder. Rap the baking trays on the work surface covered with a kitchen cloth. Leave to stand for 30 minutes until a skin forms on the surface.

Preheat the fan oven to 180°C. Put the baking trays in the oven. Bake for 12 minutes, briefly opening and shutting the oven door twice during cooking time. Take the shells out of the oven and slide them on to the work surface.

For the chocolate ganache. Cut the butter into pieces. Chop up the chocolate and tip it into a bowl. Bring the cream to the boil. Pour it over the chopped chocolate a third at a time.

Don't worry if the cream separates when you pour in the hot cream. This is caused by molecules of fat in the cream and chocolate separating. Keep mixing, continue to follow the instructions of the recipe and you will obtain a thick, glossy ganache.

When the mixture reaches 50°C, add the pieces of butter a few at a time.

Whisk to obtain a smooth ganache.

Pour it into a gratin dish. Press clingfilm over the surface of the ganache and set aside in the fridge for the ganache to thicken.

Spoon the ganache into a piping bag with a plain nozzle. Pipe a generous mound of ganache on to half the shells. Top them with the remaining shells.

Store the macarons in the fridge for 24 hours. Remove from the fridge two hours before eating.

ROSE MACARON

THIS WAS ONE OF MY FIRST CREATIONS AT FAUCHON IN 1986. I HAD RECENTLY DISCOVERED THE USE OF ROSE IN BULGARIAN SPECIALITIES, BOTH SWEET AND SAVOURY. IT GAVE ME THE IDEA FOR THE ISPAHAN BISCUIT (ROSE, LYCHEE AND RASPBERRY), WHICH CAME TO FRUITION 11 YEARS LATER. THIS IS ONE OF THE FEW MACARONS I FILL WITH BUTTER CREAM.

Makes about 72 macarons
(144 shells)

PREPARATION TIME:

about 1 hour

COOKING TIME:

about 30 minutes

STANDING TIME:

30 minutes

REFRIGERATION:

24 hours

FOR THE MACARON SHELLS

300g ground almonds

300g icing sugar

110g 'liquefied' egg whites
(see page 11)

About 5g red food
colouring

+

300g caster sugar

75g mineral water

110g 'liquefied' egg whites
(see page 11)

FOR THE ROSE BUTTER
CREAM

200g caster sugar

75g mineral water

150g whole eggs

90g egg yolk

400g very soft butter

4g rose essence (from
health food stores or
the chemist)

50g rose syrup

When you bring the sugar and water to the boil for the rose butter cream, sugar particles will spit and stick to the edge of the pan, so to cook the sugar perfectly, it is essential to brush them off with a pastry brush dipped in water.

Sift together the icing sugar and ground almonds. Stir the food colouring into the first portion of liquefied egg whites. Pour them into the bowl of icing sugar and ground almonds but do not stir.

Bring the sugar and water to boil at 118°C. When the syrup reaches 115°C, simultaneously start whisking the second portion of liquefied egg whites to soft peaks.

When the sugar reaches 118°C, pour it over the egg whites. Whisk and allow the meringue to cool down to 50°C, then fold it into the mixture of ground almonds and icing sugar. Spoon the batter into a piping bag fitted with a plain nozzle.

Pipe rounds of batter about 3.5 cm in diameter, 2 cm apart on baking trays lined with baking parchment. Leave to stand for at least 30 minutes until a skin forms on the surface.

Preheat the fan oven to 180°C. Put the baking trays in the oven. Bake for 12 minutes, briefly opening and shutting the oven door twice during cooking time. Take the shells out of the oven and slide them on to the work surface.

For the rose butter cream. Bring the sugar and water to the boil in a saucepan. When it boils, clean the sides of the pan with a damp pastry brush. Heat the sugar to 120°C.

In a bowl, whisk the eggs and egg yolks until they lighten in colour. Pour in the hot sugar at 120°C and continue whisking until it has cooled down completely.

Cream then whisk the butter in the bowl of the electric mixer until it thickens. Add the egg mixture and continue whisking to obtain a smooth consistency, then add the rose essence and rose syrup. Smooth the butter cream by whisking it briskly.

Immediately, spoon the cream into a piping bag fitted with a plain nozzle. Pipe a generous mound of ganache on to half the shells. Top them with the remaining shells. Store the macarons in the fridge for 24 hours. Remove from the fridge two hours before eating.

PIETRA MACARON

Makes about 72 macarons
   (or about 144 shells)

PREPARATION TIME:

about 1 hour

COOKING TIME:

about 35 minutes

STANDING TIME:

30 minutes

REFRIGERATION:

24 hours

FOR THE MACARON SHELLS

150g ground almonds

150g ground hazelnuts

300g icing sugar

110g 'liquefied' egg whites
   (see page 11)

+

300g caster sugar

75g mineral water

110g 'liquefied' egg whites
   (see page 11)

FOR THE PRALINE

250g whole hazelnuts with
   their skins

40g mineral water

½ vanilla pod

250g 'La Viette' butter
   (sweet butter from
   Charentes) at room
   temperature

For the caramelised hazelnuts. Preheat the oven to 170°C. Spread 250g + 60g hazelnuts evenly on the baking tray. Slide it into the oven and roast the nuts for about 15 minutes.

Put the hot nuts in a wide-mesh sieve (or a colander). Roll the nuts around to remove the skins. Put 60g nuts into a plastic bag. Crush them into little pieces with a rolling pin. Put them aside to be used to finish. Keep the rest of the nuts warm in the oven with the heat turned off.

Bring the 40g mineral water to the boil with the 150g sugar and the split vanilla pod with the seeds scraped out. When the syrup reaches 121°C, add the warm hazelnuts. Take the mixture off the heat and stir until the sugar resembles sand, then return it to the heat. Allow the nuts to caramelise, stirring constantly until the caramel turns a dark amber colour. Pour them out on to a baking tray. Remove the vanilla pod and allow the nuts to cool. Crush them finely to obtain the caramelised ground hazelnuts.

For the macaron shells. Sift together the icing sugar, ground almonds and ground hazelnuts then pour one portion of the liquefied egg whites over them but do not stir.

Bring the water and sugar to boil at 118°C. When the syrup reaches 115°C, simultaneously start whisking the second portion of liquefied egg whites to soft peaks. When the sugar reaches 118°C, pour it over the egg whites. Whisk and allow the meringue to cool down to 50°C, then fold it into the mixture of nuts and icing sugar. Spoon the batter into a piping bag fitted with a plain nozzle.

Pipe rounds of batter about 3.5 cm in diameter, spacing them 2 cm apart on baking trays lined with parchment. Lightly sprinkle with the crushed roasted hazelnuts.

THE FRAGRANCE OF CARAMELISING HAZELNUTS IS FOREVER ASSOCIATED WITH MY CHILD-HOOD. MY FATHER, GEORGES HERMÉ, A BAKER AND PASTRY CHEF IN COLMAR, USED TO MAKE CARAMELISED HAZELNUT PASTE FOR HIS CHOCOLATES.

100g 'liquefied' egg
    whites (see page 11)
160g caster sugar
40g mineral water

60g whole hazelnuts
    with their skins

You need to beat the butter for a long time without heating it to make it light and frothy.

Rap the baking trays on the work surface covered with a kitchen cloth. Leave the shells to stand for at least 30 minutes until they form a skin.

Preheat the fan oven to 180°C then slide the trays into the oven. Bake for 12 minutes quickly opening and shutting the oven door twice during cooking time. Out of the oven, slide the shells on to the work surface.

For the praline. Whisk the egg whites to peaks in the electric mixer. Meanwhile, bring the 40g water to boil with the 160g sugar. When the sugar reaches 121°C, pour it over the egg whites and whisk until the meringue has completely cooled.

Beat the butter for 5 minutes in the electric mixer fitted with the paddle attachment then add the caramelised ground hazelnuts a little at a time. Beat for 5 minutes.

Carefully add a third of the meringue to the praline mixture then add the rest, stirring delicately.

Spoon the praline into the piping bag fitted with a plain nozzle. Pipe a generous mound of cream on to half the shells. Top with the remaining shells.

Store the macarons for 24 hours in the fridge and bring back out two hours before serving.

BLACKCURRANT MACARON

Makes about 72 macarons
(or about 144 shells)

PREPARATION TIME:

the day before, 10 minutes;
the same day, about 1
hour.

COOKING TIME:

the day before, a few
minutes; the same day,
about 20 minutes

STANDING TIME:

30 minutes

REFRIGERATION TIME:

4 hours + 24 hours

FOR THE MACARON SHELLS

300g ground almonds

300g icing sugar

110g 'liquefied' egg whites
(see page 11)

15g titanium oxide diluted
in 10g warm mineral
water

3 drops blue food
colouring

10g approx. carmine red
food colouring

+

300g caster sugar

75g mineral water

110g 'liquefied' egg whites
(see page 11)

FOR THE BLACKCURRANT
GANACHE

400g Valrhona Ivoire
couverture or white
chocolate

400g fresh or frozen
blackcurrants

I add redcurrants to take
the edge off the tartness
of the blackcurrants and
enliven the flavour with
a tangy hint.

The titanium oxide
powder for whitening is
optional. It is added to
give the macarons a
lighter colour, but if you
prefer not to use it, you
should reduce the
quantities of food
colouring.

The day before, prepare the blackcurrants for the ganache and to finish. If you are using frozen blackcurrants, tip the 400g into a colander to defrost.

Still the day before, bring the 200g water to boil with the sugar. Tip the 200g fresh or frozen blackcurrants into the boiling syrup. Bring it back to the boil, then remove from the heat and allow the fruit to macerate until next day.

Next day, prepare the macarons. Sift together the icing sugar and ground almonds.

Dilute the titanium oxide in a bowl of warm water and stir it with the food colouring into the liquefied egg whites. Pour them over the icing sugar-almond mixture but do not stir.

Bring the water and sugar to boil at 118°C. When the syrup reaches 115°C, simultaneously start whisking the second portion of liquefied egg whites to soft peaks on a medium speed.

When the sugar reaches 118°C, pour it over the egg whites. Whisk and allow the meringue to cool down to 50°C, then fold it into the almond-sugar mixture. Spoon the batter into a piping bag with a plain nozzle.

Pipe rounds of batter about 3.5 cm in diameter, spacing them 2 cm apart on baking trays lined with parchment. Rap the baking trays on the work surface covered with a kitchen cloth. Allow the shells to stand for at least 30 minutes until they form a skin.

Preheat the fan oven to 180°C then put the trays in the oven. Bake for 12 minutes quickly opening and shutting the oven door twice during cooking time. Out of the oven, slide the shells on to the work surface.

For the blackcurrant ganache. Strip the redcurrants from the stalks. Blend the 400g fresh or defrosted blackcurrants with the redcurrants then put them through the vegetable mill or centrifugal juicer. Bring the juice obtained to the boil.

Chop up the white chocolate and melt it in a bowl over a saucepan of barely simmering water. Pour the hot juice over

130g redcurrants (or
  raspberries)

FOR THE FILLING

200g fresh or frozen
  blackcurrants

200g water

100g caster sugar

the chocolate a third at a time.

Transfer the mixture to a gratin dish. Press clingfilm over the surface of the ganache and set aside in the fridge for the ganache to thicken.

Drain the blackcurrants then pat dry using kitchen roll an hour before filling the macarons.

Spoon the ganache into the piping bag with a plain nozzle. Pipe a generous mound of the ganache on to half the shells. Press 2 or 3 blackcurrants gently into the centre of the ganache. Top with the remaining shells.

Store the macarons for 24 hours in the fridge and bring back out two hours before serving.

I CREATED THIS MACARON AT THE REQUEST OF A CLIENT. I THINK BLACKCURRANTS HAVE A UNIQUE FLAVOUR AND I INITIALLY LIMITED THE MACARON TO PIERRE HERMÉ IN TOKYO BEFORE MAKING IT AVAILABLE IN PARIS.

SALTED-BUTTER CARAMEL MACARON

I PUSH THE CARAMELISATION OF SUGAR TO ITS LIMITS TO OBTAIN A STRONG CARAMEL FLAVOUR AND GIVE IT A FINE DARK AMBER COLOUR. I PREFER A BUTTER-BASED CREAM BECAUSE IT BRINGS OUT THE TASTE OF CARAMELISED SUGAR.

Makes about 72 macarons (or about 144 shells)

PREPARATION TIME:

about 1 hour

COOKING TIME:

about 30 minutes

STANDING TIME:

30 minutes

REFRIGERATION TIME:

24 hours

FOR THE MACARON SHELLS

300g ground almonds

300g icing sugar

110g 'liquefied' egg whites (see page 11)

15g Trablit coffee extract

15g egg yellow food colouring

+

300g caster sugar

75g mineral water

110g 'liquefied' egg whites (see page 11)

FOR THE SALTED-BUTTER CARAMEL CREAM

300g caster sugar

335g liquid crème fraîche or whipping cream (35% fat)

65g lightly salted 'La Viette' butter (sweet butter from Charentes)

+

290g softened La Viette butter

The butter is soft enough when you can dip a finger in without meeting any resistance. Make sure you take the butter out of the fridge several hours in advance.

Sift together the icing sugar and ground almonds. Stir the coffee extract and food colouring into the first portion of liquefied egg whites. Pour them over the mixture of ground almonds and icing sugar but do not stir.

Bring the water and sugar to boil to 118°C. When the syrup reaches 115°C, simultaneously start whisking the second portion of liquefied egg whites to soft peaks on a medium speed. When the sugar reaches 118°C, pour it over the egg whites. Whisk and allow the meringue to cool down to 50°C, then fold it into the sugar-almond mixture. Spoon the batter into a piping bag with a plain nozzle.

Pipe rounds of batter about 3.5 cm in diameter, spacing them 2 cm apart on baking trays lined with baking parchment. Allow the shells to stand for at least 30 minutes until they form a skin.

Preheat the fan oven to 180°C then put the baking trays into the oven. Bake for 12 minutes quickly opening and shutting the oven door twice during cooking time. Out of the oven, slide the shells on to the work surface.

For the salted-butter caramel cream. Bring the liquid crème fraîche or whipping cream (35% fat) to the boil. Tip about 50g sugar into a large saucepan and allow it to melt then add another 50g sugar and continue four more times.

Allow the syrup to caramelise until it turns a very dark amber colour. Take the pan off the heat and add the 65g lightly salted butter, taking care as the cream may bubble and spit. Stir with a spatula then pour in the cream a little at a time, stirring constantly. Put the saucepan back on a low heat and continue heating until the cream reaches 108°C. Pour it into a gratin dish and press clingfilm over the surface. Set aside in the fridge until cool. Beat the 290g softened butter for 8 to 10 minutes then add the cream half at a time. Spoon the salted-butter caramel cream straight into a piping bag with a plain nozzle.

Pipe a generous mound of filling on to half the macaron shells. Top with the remaining shells.

Store the macarons for 24 hours in the fridge and bring back out two hours before serving.

PISTACHIO MACARON

ON ITS OWN, PISTACHIO HAS A DELICATE FLAVOUR THAT NEEDS TO BE EMPHASISED WITH A LITTLE BITTER ALMOND EXTRACT. I LIKE THE DIFFERENT FLAVOURS OF ROASTED PISTACHIO AND BITTER ALMOND.

Makes about 72 macarons
(or about 144 shells)

PREPARATION TIME:

about 1 hour

COOKING TIME:

about 20 minutes

STANDING TIME:

30 minutes

REFRIGERATION TIME:

4 hours + 24 hours

FOR THE MACARON SHELLS

300g ground almonds

300g icing sugar

110g 'liquefied' egg whites
(see page 11)

2g approx. lemon yellow
food colouring

4g approx. pistachio green
food colouring

+

300g caster sugar

75g mineral water

110g 'liquefied' egg whites
(see page 11)

FOR THE PISTACHIO
GANACHE

300g liquid crème fraîche
or whipping cream
(35% fat)

300g Valrhona Ivoire
couverture or white
chocolate

45g pistachio paste (or 45g
unsalted shelled
pistachios blended with
the cream)

1 or 2 drops bitter almond
essence

I use two pistachio pastes. One is pure and brownish in colour; the other is greener with an aroma of bitter almonds. If you are only using pure pistachio paste, add a few drops of bitter almond essence to bring out the flavour of the pistachio, and do the same if you are using unsalted shelled pistachios.

Sift together the icing sugar and ground almonds. Stir the colourings into the first portion of liquefied egg whites. Pour them over the mixture of icing sugar and ground almonds but do not stir.

Bring the water and sugar to boil at 118°C. When the syrup reaches 115°C, simultaneously start whisking the second portion of liquefied egg whites to soft peaks on a medium speed.

When the sugar reaches 118°C, pour it over the egg whites. Whisk and allow the meringue to cool down to 50°C, then fold it into the almond-sugar mixture. Spoon the batter into a piping bag with a plain nozzle.

Pipe rounds of batter about 3.5 cm in diameter, spacing them 2 cm apart on baking trays lined with baking parchment.

Rap the tray on the work surface covered with a kitchen cloth. Leave to stand for at least 30 minutes until a skin forms on the shells.

Preheat the fan oven to 180°C then put the trays in the oven. Bake for 12 minutes quickly opening and shutting the oven door twice during cooking time. Out of the oven, slide the shells on to the work surface.

For the pistachio ganache. Chop up the chocolate and melt it in a bowl over a pan of barely simmering water.

Bring the cream to the boil with the pistachio paste. Stir then pour it over the chocolate a third at a time.

Blend for 10 minutes with a hand blender. Pour the ganache into a gratin dish. Press clingfilm over the surface of the ganache and set aside in the fridge for the ganache to thicken.

Spoon the ganache into a piping bag with a plain nozzle. Pipe a generous mound of ganache on to half of the shells then top with the remaining shells.

Store the macarons in the fridge for 24 hours and bring them back out 2 hours before serving.

COFFEE MACARON

Makes about 72 macarons
(or about 144 shells)

PREPARATION TIME:

about 1 hour

COOKING TIME:

about 20 minutes

STANDING TIME:

30 minutes

REFRIGERATION TIME:

2 hours + 24 hours

FOR THE MACARON SHELLS

300g ground almonds

300g icing sugar

175g 'liquefied' egg whites
(see page 11)

30g Trablit coffee extract

+

500g caster sugar

125g mineral water

135g 'liquefied' egg whites
(see page 11)

FOR THE COFFEE GANACHE

400g liquid crème fraîche
or whipping cream (35%
fat)

400g Valrhona Ivoire
couverture or white
chocolate

20g ground coffee
(Colombian or Ethiopian
Mocca)

Sift together the icing sugar and ground almonds. Stir the coffee extract into the first portion of liquefied egg whites. Pour them over the mixture of icing sugar and ground almonds but do not stir.

Bring the water and sugar to boil at 118°C. When the syrup reaches 115°C, simultaneously start whisking the second portion of liquefied egg whites to soft peaks.

When the sugar reaches 118°C, pour it over the egg whites. Whisk and allow the meringue to cool down to 50°C, then fold it into the almond-sugar mixture. Spoon the batter into a piping bag with a plain nozzle.

Pipe rounds of batter about 3.5 cm in diameter, spacing them 2 cm apart on baking trays lined with baking parchment.

Rap the tray on the work surface covered with a kitchen cloth. Leave to stand for at least 30 minutes until a skin forms on the shells.

Preheat the fan oven to 180°C then slide the trays into the oven. Bake for 12 minutes quickly opening and shutting the oven door twice during cooking time. Out of the oven, slide the shells on to the work surface.

For the coffee ganache. Chop up the chocolate and melt it in a bowl over a saucepan of barely simmering water. Bring the cream to the boil. Add the ground coffee. Remove from the heat and cover. Allow to infuse for a few minutes then strain it through a fine-mesh sieve. Pour the hot infused cream over the chocolate a third at a time. Stir to obtain a smooth ganache.

Transfer the ganache to a gratin dish. Press clingfilm over the surface of the ganache and set aside in the fridge for the ganache to thicken.

Get hold of good quality Ivory couverture rather than ordinary bars of white chocolate: the coffee filling will be better.

Spoon the ganache into a piping bag with a plain nozzle. Pipe a generous mound of the ganache on to half the shells and top with the remaining shells.

Store the macarons in the fridge for 24 hours and bring them back out 2 hours before serving.

WHEN I WAS AN APPRENTICE, MACARONS WERE TRADITIONALLY FILLED WITH FLAVOURED BUTTER CREAM USING INSTANT COFFEE AND COFFEE EXTRACT. I WANTED MY GANACHE TO TASTE OF REAL COFFEE, SOMETHING LIKE A GENUINE ESPRESSO. SO, I INFUSE GROUND COFFEE IN BOILING CREAM THEN I STRAIN IT AND ADD THE WHITE CHOCOLATE FOR A DELICIOUSLY POWERFUL COFFEE FLAVOUR.

RASPBERRY MACARON

Makes about 72 macarons
(or about 144 shells)

PREPARATION TIME:

about 1 hour

COOKING TIME:

30 minutes

STANDING TIME:

30 minutes

REFRIGERATION TIME:

24 hours

FOR THE RASPBERRY JAM

1kg fresh or frozen
    raspberries

600g caster sugar

15g pectin (or a sachet)

50g lemon juice

FOR THE MACARON SHELLS

300g ground almonds

300g icing sugar

110g 'liquefied' egg whites
    (see page 11)

22g raspberry red food
    colouring

+

300g caster sugar

75g mineral water

110g 'liquefied' egg
    whites (see page 11)

Start by making the raspberry jam. Blend the raspberries for 10 minutes using a hand blender.

Tip them into a saucepan with the sugar and pectin. Bring to the boil on a very high heat then boil for 4 to 5 minutes. Add the lemon juice and stir.

Pour the jam into a gratin dish. Allow to cool and set aside in the fridge. Sift together the icing sugar and ground almonds. Stir the food colouring into the first portion of liquefied egg whites. Pour them over the mixture of icing sugar and ground almonds but do not stir.

Bring the water and sugar to boil at 118°C. When the syrup reaches 115°C, simultaneously start whisking the second portion of liquefied egg whites to soft peaks.

When the sugar reaches 118°C, pour it over the egg whites. Whisk and allow the meringue to cool down to 50°C, then fold it into the almond-sugar mixture. Spoon the batter into a piping bag with a plain nozzle.

Pipe rounds of batter about 3.5 cm in diameter, spacing them 2 cm apart on baking trays lined with baking parchment.

Rap the tray on the work surface covered with a kitchen cloth. Leave to stand for at least 30 minutes until a skin forms on the shells.

Preheat the fan oven to 180°C then slide the trays into the oven. Bake for 12 minutes quickly opening and shutting the oven door twice during cooking time. Out of the oven, slide the shells on to the work surface.

Spoon the raspberry jam into a piping bag with a plain nozzle. Pipe a generous mound of jam on to half the shells and top with the remaining shells.

Store the macarons in the fridge for 24 hours and bring them back out 2 hours before serving.

The raspberry jam should be made several days in advance. Blend it thoroughly to break up the pips and release the pectin in the fruit. You can keep any leftover jam for a breakfast treat.

THIS IS THE RECIPE AS I WAS TAUGHT IT 32 YEARS AGO WHEN I WAS AN APPRENTICE. ITS SWEET RASPBERRY JAM FILLING MAKES IT A MACARON THAT WILL EVOKE THE SUGARY FLAVOURS WE LOVED AS CHILDREN.

LEMON MACARON

THE CLASSIC LEMON MACARON WAS ONE OF MY FIRST CREATIVE INI-
TIATIVES. I LIKE TO USE JUICY MENTON LEMONS; THE ZEST IS DELI-
CIOUSLY TANGY AND COMBINES WITH THEIR SUAVE AROMA TO
CREATE A WONDERFUL MOMENT OF PURE GASTRONOMIC PLEASURE.

Makes about 72 macarons (or about 144 shells)

PREPARATION TIME:

the day before, 15 minutes; the next day, about 1 hour

COOKING TIME:

about 20 minutes

STANDING TIME:

30 minutes

REFRIGERATION TIME:

2 hours + 24 hours

FOR THE MACARON SHELLS

300g ground almonds

300g icing sugar

110g 'liquefied' egg whites (see page 11)

½ g approx. golden yellow food colouring (½ coffee spoon)

10g lemon yellow food colouring

+

300g caster sugar

75g mineral water

110g 'liquefied' egg whites (see page 11)

FOR THE LEMON CREAM

225g whole fresh eggs

240g caster sugar

8g zest of Menton lemons (or untreated organic lemons)

160g fresh lemon juice

350g 'La Viette' butter (sweet butter from Charentes) at room temperature

100g ground almonds

The day before, make the lemon cream. Rinse, dry and zest the lemons. Rub the zest and sugar together between your hands.

In a bowl, mix together the lemon juice, the lemon and sugar mixture and the eggs. Tip this into a bowl over a saucepan of barely simmering water. Beat until the mixture reaches 83/84°C. Allow to cool to 60°C, then add the butter cut into pieces. Whisk until the cream is smooth then use a hand blender to blend for 10 minutes.

Pour the cream into a gratin dish. Press clingfilm over the surface of the cream. Set aside in the fridge until next day.

Next day, sift together the icing sugar and ground almonds. Stir the food colouring into the first portion of liquefied egg whites. Pour them over the mixture of icing sugar and ground almonds but do not stir.

Bring the water and sugar to boil at 118°C. When the syrup reaches 115°C, simultaneously start whisking the second portion of liquefied egg whites to soft peaks.

When the sugar reaches 118°C, pour it over the egg whites. Whisk and allow the meringue to cool down to 50°C, then fold it into the almond-sugar mixture.

Spoon the batter into a piping bag with a plain nozzle.

Pipe rounds of batter about 3.5 cm in diameter, spacing them 2 cm apart on baking trays lined with baking parchment.

Rap the trays on the work surface covered with a kitchen cloth. Leave to stand for at least 30 minutes until a skin forms on the surface.

Preheat the fan oven to 180°C then put the trays in the oven. Bake for 12 minutes quickly opening and shutting the oven door twice during cooking time. Out of the oven, slide the shells on to the work surface.

I recommend using a Microplane grater to zest the lemons as finely as possible. Rub together the sugar and lemon zest thoroughly between the palms of your hands, wearing disposable gloves.

Stir together the lemon cream and ground almonds. Spoon the cream into a piping bag with a plain nozzle. Pipe a generous mound of cream on to half the shells and top with the remaining shells.

Store the macarons in the fridge for 24 hours and bring them back out 2 hours before serving.

MARRONS GLACÉS MACARON

I WANTED TO CAPTURE THE DELICATE BITTERNESS AND MELTING CONSISTENCY OF MARRONS GLACÉS IN THE SMOOTH, VELVETY TEXTURE OF A MACARON.

Makes about 72 macarons
(or about 144 shells)

PREPARATION TIME

about 1 hour

COOKING TIME:

about 20 minutes

STANDING TIME:

30 minutes

REFRIGERATION TIME:

24 hours

FOR THE MACARON
SHELLS

300g ground almonds

300g icing sugar

15g cacao pâte (or dark
chocolate, 100% cocoa
solids)

30g chestnut purée

105g 'liquefied' egg whites
(see page 11)

3g approx. carmine red
food colouring

+

300g caster sugar

75g mineral water

115g 'liquefied' egg whites
(see page 11)

FOR THE MARRONS
GLACÉS CREAM

210g chestnut purée

110g chestnut paste

160g 'La Viette' butter
(sweet butter from
Charentes) at room
temperature

10g old 'JM' brown rum
'agricole'

130g marrons glacés
crumbs

Make sure you crush the marrons glacés crumbs finely so that you don't block the nozzle when piping the cream on to the shells.

Sift together the icing sugar and ground almonds. Chop up the cacao pâte and melt it at 50°C in a bowl over a saucepan of barely simmering water. Stir the chestnut purée and the food colouring into the first portion of liquefied egg whites. Add them to the mixture of icing sugar and ground almonds but do not stir.

Bring the water and sugar to boil at 118°C. When the syrup reaches 115°C, simultaneously start whisking the second portion of liquefied egg whites to soft peaks.

When the sugar reaches 118°C, pour it over the egg whites. Whisk and allow the meringue to cool down to 50°C, add it to the almond-sugar mixture and stir, then fold in the melted cacao. Spoon the batter into a piping bag with a plain nozzle.

Pipe rounds of batter about 3.5 cm in diameter, spacing them 2 cm apart on baking trays lined with baking parchment.

Rap the trays on the work surface covered with a kitchen cloth. Leave to stand for at least 30 minutes until a skin forms on the shells.

Preheat the fan oven to 180°C then put the trays in the oven. Bake for 12 minutes quickly opening and shutting the oven door twice during cooking time. Out of the oven, slide the shells on to the work surface.

For the marrons glacés cream. Rinse the marrons glacés crumbs in warm water. Drain and dry them, then chop them finely.

Crumble the chestnut paste into the rum with the chestnut purée. Beat in the mixer fitted with the paddle attachment, then remove the mixture obtained.

In the bowl of the electric mixer fitted with the paddle attachment, beat the butter to a creamy consistency. Add the chestnut mixture. Beat for another 8 to 10 minutes. Add the marrons glacés crumbs. Beat for 1 minute. Spoon the chestnut butter cream straight into a piping bag with a plain nozzle.

Pipe a generous mound of cream on to half the shells and top with the remaining shells.

Store the macarons in the fridge for 24 hours and bring them back out 2 hours before serving.

FETISH
MACARONS

'PIERRE HERMÉ HOUSE "FETISH" FLAVOURS THAT ARE CLOSE TO MY HEART.'

INFINITELY CHOCOLATE MACARON

Extra-bitter chocolate, cocoa nibs and fleur de sel chocolate chips

Makes about 72 macarons (or about 144 shells)

PREPARATION TIME:

about 1 hour 30 minutes

COOKING TIME:

about 25 minutes

STANDING TIME:

30 minutes

REFRIGERATION TIME:

3 hours + 24 hours

FOR THE DARK FLEUR DE SEL CHOCOLATE CHIPS

100g Valrhona Araguani chocolate or dark chocolate with 70% cocoa solids

2g fleur de sel

FOR THE MACARON SHELLS

120g cacao pâte or dark chocolate, 100% cocoa solids

300g ground almonds

300g icing sugar

110g 'liquefied' egg whites (see page 11)

Start by making the fleur de sel chocolate chips. Crush the fleur de sel with a rolling pin.

Chop up the chocolate using a serrated knife and melt it in a bowl over a saucepan of barely simmering water, but don't let it get too hot. Stir the crushed fleur de sel into the chocolate. Pour the chocolate on to a sheet of plastic (the sort used for dividers).

Use a spatula to spread out a fine layer of chocolate, cover with a second sheet of plastic and place a weight over the whole surface so that the chocolate holds its shape. Set aside in the fridge for 3 hours. Break it up into tiny chips. Set them aside in the fridge. It is best to temper the chocolate though it is not essential because the chocolate chips will not be visible.

For the macarons. Sift together the icing sugar and ground almonds. Chop up the cacao pâte and melt it at 50°C in a bowl over a pan of barely simmering water. Pour the food colouring into the first portion of liquefied egg whites. Add them to the icing sugar-ground almond mixture but do not stir.

Bring the water and sugar to the boil at 118°C. When the syrup reaches 115°C, simultaneously start whisking the second portion of liquefied egg whites. When the sugar reaches 118°C, pour it over the egg whites. Whisk and allow the meringue to cool down to 50°C, add it to the almond-sugar mixture and stir, then fold in the melted cacao.

Spoon the batter into a piping bag fitted with a plain nozzle. Pipe rounds of batter 3.5 cm in diameter, spacing them 2 cm apart on baking trays lined with baking parchment. Rap the trays on the work surface covered with a kitchen cloth. Leave to stand for at least 30 minutes until a skin forms on the shells. (Cont.)

WHAT A TREAT THE NAME PROMISES! CHOCOLATE, ONLY CHOCOLATE AND NOTHING BUT CHOCOLATE! 'INFINITELY CHOCOLATE' WAS INSPIRED BY THE ORGANIZATION CARRÉMENT CHOCOLAT FOUNDED BY MY FRIEND CHLOÉ DOUTRE-ROUSSEL.

4.5g carmine red food
   colouring

+

330g caster sugar

75g mineral water

110g 'liquefied' egg
   whites (see page 11)

FOR THE CHOCOLATE
GANACHE

400g liquid crème
   fraîche or whipping
   cream (35% fat)

90g Valrhona Araguani
   couverture

160g cacao pâte (or
   dark chocolate,
   100% cocoa solids)

90g 'La Viette' butter
   (sweet butter from
   Charentes) at room
   temperature

70g cocoa nibs

When you have crushed the fleur de sel with a rolling pin, I recommend you sift it and use only the tiny, sifted crystals, discarding the ones that are left in the sieve.

Preheat the fan oven to 180°C then put the trays in the oven. Bake for 12 minutes quickly opening and shutting the oven door twice during cooking time. Out of the oven, slide the shells on to the work surface.

For the ganache. Cut the butter into pieces. Chop up the cacao pâte and chocolate finely using a serrated knife. Bring the cream to the boil then pour it over the chopped chocolate a third at a time.

When the chocolate reaches 35 to 40°C, gently stir in the pieces of butter a few at a time and the cocoa nibs.

Pour the ganache into a gratin dish. Press clingfilm over the surface of the ganache, then set aside in the fridge for the ganache to thicken.

Pour the ganache into a piping bag fitted with a plain nozzle. Pipe a generous mound of ganache on to half the shells, scatter 3 or 4 fleur de sel chocolate chips on top and cover with the remaining shells.

Store in the fridge for 24 hours until serving.

CÉLESTE MACARON

Strawberry, rhubarb and passion fruit

Makes about 72
  macarons (or about
  144 shells)

PREPARATION TIME:

The day before, 20
  minutes; next day, 1
  hour

COOKING TIME:

about 1 hour

STANDING TIME:

30 minutes

REFRIGERATION TIME:

2 hours + 24 hours

FOR THE MACARON
SHELLS

300g ground almonds

300g icing sugar

110g 'liquefied' egg
  whites (see page 11)

5g approx. lemon yellow
  food colouring

½ g approx. red food
  colouring (½ coffee
  spoon)

+

300g caster sugar

75g mineral water

110g 'liquefied' egg
  whites (see page 11)

FOR THE RHUBARB JAM

200g fresh or frozen
  rhubarb

30g caster sugar

1 small pinch ground
  cloves

The day before, prepare the rhubarb jam. Cut the rhubarb into chunks and put them in the sugar to macerate.

Still the day before, halve the passion fruits and scoop out the seeds with a teaspoon. Strain the fruit to obtain 105g juice. In a bowl, stir together the passion fruit juice with the eggs, lemon juice and sugar. Put the mixture in a bowl over a pan of barely simmering water. Whisk until the mixture reaches 83 to 84°C.

Allow to cool to about 60°C. Cut the butter into pieces then add them to the mixture and blend for 10 minutes with a hand blender. Store in the fridge until next day.

Next day, drain the rhubarb. Cook it with a pinch of cloves for about 8 minutes to obtain a purée. Allow to cool. Blend with a hand blender. Weigh out 150g of the rhubarb jam.

Soak the gelatine leaves for 15 minutes in cold water to soften. Rinse and dry the strawberries. Remove the stalks. Blend the strawberries and sugar to a purée with a hand blender. Drain and dry the gelatine then add it to the 150g hot rhubarb and stir in the strawberry purée. Pour into a gratin dish lined with clingfilm to a depth of 4 mm. Allow to cool for 1 hour in the fridge then put the dish in the freezer for 2 hours. Turn out the jelly and cut it into 1.5 cm squares. Return the jelly squares to the freezer.

For the coloured sugar. Preheat the oven to 60°C. Put on disposable gloves. Mix the sugar with a few drops of food colouring and rub it between the palms of your hands. Spread out the coloured sugar on a baking tray. Slide the tray into the oven and dry the sugar for at least 30 minutes.

For the macaron shells. Sift together the icing sugar and ground almonds. Stir the food colouring into the first portion of liquefied egg whites and pour them over the mixture of icing sugar and ground almonds do not stir.

Bring the water and sugar to boil at 118°C. When the syrup reaches 115°C, simultaneously start whisking the second portion of liquefied egg whites to soft peaks.

When the sugar reaches 118°C, pour it over the egg whites. Whisk and allow the meringue to cool down to

You can enjoy any leftover rhubarb jam with a fromage blanc or plain yogurt.

FOR THE RHUBARB
AND STRAWBERRY
COMPOTE

150g stewed rhubarb

450g strawberries
(Mara des bois or
Gariguettes)

20g caster sugar

45g mineral water

3g gelatine leaves

FOR THE PASSION
FRUIT CREAM

150g eggs

140g caster sugar

4 to 5 passion fruits
(for 105g juice)

15g lemon juice

150g 'La Viette' butter
(sweet butter from
Charentes) at room
temperature

FOR THE PASSION
FRUIT MOUSSELINE

500g Passion Fruit
Cream

150g 'La Viette' butter
at room temperature

TO FINISH

100g granulated sugar

A few drops red food
colouring

or

Edible ruby glitter (see
page 205)

50°C, then fold it into the almond-sugar mixture. Spoon the batter into a piping bag fitted with a plain nozzle. Pipe rounds of batter about 3.5 cm in diameter, spacing them 2 cm apart on baking trays lined with baking parchment.

Rap the baking trays on the work surface covered with a kitchen cloth. Sprinkle with pinches of coloured sugar (or ruby glitter). Leave the shells to stand for at least 30 minutes until they form a skin.

Preheat the fan oven to 180°C. Put the trays in the oven and bake for 12 minutes quickly opening and shutting the oven door twice during cooking time. Out of the oven, slide the shells on to the work surface.

For the passion fruit mousseline. In the bowl of an electric mixer fitted with the paddle attachment, beat the 150g butter for 10 minutes then add the passion fruit cream you prepared the day before, a little at a time. Blend to a smooth cream.

Pour the cream into a piping bag fitted with a plain nozzle. Pipe a generous mound of cream on to half the shells. Lightly press a square of frozen jelly into the centre and finish with a dot of cream. Top with the remaining shells.

Store the macarons for 24 hours in the fridge and bring back out at the point of serving.

THE IDEA FOR THIS MACARON CAME FROM THE PAIRING OF RHUBARB AND STRAWBERRY, A FAVOURITE IN GERMANY. THEN I ADDED PASSION FRUIT AND GAVE THE RESULTING CAKE THE EVOCATIVE NAME 'CÉLESTE'. THE MACARONS ARE FILLED WITH A SQUARE OF RHUBARB AND STRAWBERRY COMPOTE AND THE TWO TANGY FLAVOURS ARE ENCASED IN A LIGHT AND SILKY PASSION FRUIT CREAM.

EDEN MACARON
Peach, apricot and saffron

Makes about 72
  macarons (or about
  144 shells)

PREPARATION TIME:

about 1 hour

COOKING TIME:

about 25 minutes

STANDING TIME:

30 minutes

REFRIGERATION:

2 hours + 24 hours

FOR THE MACARON
SHELLS

300g ground almonds

300g icing sugar

110g 'liquefied' egg
  whites (see page 11)

4g approx. yellow food
  colouring

4g approx. red food
  colouring

+

300g caster sugar

75g mineral water

110g 'liquefied' egg
  whites (see page 11)

Sift together the icing sugar and ground almonds. Stir the food colouring into the first portion of liquefied egg whites. Pour them over the mixture of icing sugar and ground almonds but do not stir.

Bring the water and sugar to boil at 118°C. When the syrup reaches 115°C, simultaneously start whisking the second portion of liquefied egg whites to soft peaks. When the sugar reaches 118°C, pour it over the egg whites. Whisk and allow the meringue to cool down to 50°C, then fold it into the almond-sugar mixture. Spoon the batter into a piping bag fitted with a plain nozzle.

Pipe rounds of batter about 3.5 cm in diameter, spacing them 2 cm apart on baking trays lined with baking parchment. Rap the baking trays on the work surface covered with a kitchen cloth. Leave the shells to stand for at least 30 minutes until they form a skin.

Preheat the fan oven to 180°C then put the trays in the oven. Bake for 12 minutes quickly opening and shutting the oven door twice during cooking time. Out of the oven, slide the shells on to the work surface.

For the peach ganache. Chop the soft apricots into 2 mm cubes. Bring the cream to the boil, then take it off the heat and add the saffron threads. Cover with a lid and allow to infuse for 10 minutes. Chop up the chocolate and melt it in a bowl over a pan of barely simmering water.

Peel the peaches. Halve them and remove the stones. Blend the apricot flesh to a purée with the lemon juice. Strain it finely. Heat the peach purée to a temperature of no more than 40°C.

Pour the heated peach purée and cream infused with saffron over the melted chocolate. Stir then add the cubes of soft apricots.

IN 1987, I CREATED A CAKE CALLED 'COEUR DE VELOURS' ('HEART OF VELVET') THAT ASSOCIA-TED SAFFRON WITH PEACHES. A FEW YEARS LATER, I ADDED A HINT OF ACIDITY TO THE COMBINATION BY INCLUDING PIECES OF SOFT APRICOT.

FOR THE GANACHE OF
PEACH WITH SAFFRON
AND SOFT APRICOTS

A dozen saffron
threads

20g liquid crème
fraîche or whipping
cream (35% fat)

350g Valrhona Ivoire
couverture or white
chocolate

450g ripe white
peaches

20g lemon juice

140g soft apricots (in a
bag on the dried
fruit aisle)

In season, flat white peaches from the Gard region of France are best for this recipe. Soft apricots have been partially rehydrated and are readily available from the dried fruit aisle in supermarkets.

Transfer the mixture to a gratin dish. Press clingfilm over the surface of the ganache, then set aside in the fridge for the ganache to thicken.

Spoon the ganache into a piping bag fitted with a plain nozzle. Pipe a generous mound of ganache on to half the shells and top with the remaining shells.

Stand the macarons for 24 hours in the fridge and bring them back out 2 hours before serving.

ISPAHAN MACARON
Lychee, rose and raspberry

Makes about 72
macarons (or about
144 shells)

PREPARATION TIME:

about 1 hour 30
minutes

COOKING TIME:

about 25 minutes

STANDING TIME:

30 minutes

REFRIGERATION:

2 hours + 24 hours

FOR THE RASPBERRY
JELLY

420g raspberries

35g caster sugar

4g gelatine leaves

FOR THE MACARON
SHELLS

300g ground almonds

300g icing sugar

110g 'liquefied' egg
whites (see page 11)

4g approx. strawberry
food colouring

4g approx. carmine red
food colouring

+

300g caster sugar

75g mineral water

110g 'liquefied' egg
whites (see page 11)

You can buy lychees fresh in season but their flavour is less pronounced than preserved lychees. I usually prefer tea to sweet wines with desserts, but I make an exception for this macaron and think the best accompaniment is a wonderful late harvested Gewurztraminer Altenbourg from the Albert Mann domaine in Alsace.

Start by preparing the raspberry jelly. Soak the gelatine leaves for 15 minutes in cold water to soften.

Using a hand blender, blend the raspberries and sugar to a purée. Strain the purée to remove the pips. Heat a quarter of the purée to 45°C. Drain and dry the gelatine and add to the hot purée. Stir and add the rest of the raspberry purée.

Pour it into a gratin dish lined with clingfilm to a depth of 4 mm. Allow to cool for 1 hour at room temperature then put the dish in the freezer for 2 hours. Turn out the jelly and cut it into 1.5 cm squares. Return the jelly squares to the freezer.

For the coloured sugar. Preheat the oven to 60°C. Put on disposable gloves. Mix the sugar with a few drops of food colouring and rub it between the palms of your hands. Spread out the coloured sugar on a baking tray. Put the tray in the oven and dry the sugar for 30 minutes.

For the shells. Sift together the icing sugar and ground almonds. Stir the food colouring into the first portion of liquefied egg whites and pour them over the mixture of icing sugar and ground almonds but do not stir.

Bring the water and sugar to boil at 118°C. When the syrup reaches 115°C, simultaneously start whisking the second portion of liquefied egg whites to soft peaks. When the sugar reaches 118°C, pour it over the egg whites. Whisk and allow the meringue to cool down to 50°C, then fold it into the almond-icing sugar mixture. Spoon the batter into a piping bag fitted with a plain nozzle.

Pipe rounds of batter about 3.5 cm in diameter, spacing them 2 cm apart on baking trays lined with baking parchment. Rap the baking trays on the work surface covered with a kitchen cloth. Sprinkle every other row with pinches of coloured sugar or ruby glitter. Leave the shells to stand for at least 30 minutes until they form a skin.

Preheat the fan oven to 180°C then put the trays in the oven. Bake for 12 minutes quickly opening and shutting the oven door twice during cooking time. Out

410g Valrhona Ivoire
couverture or white
chocolate

400g lychees (preserved
in syrup)

60g liquid crème
fraîche or whipping
cream (35% fat)

3g rose essence (from
the delicatessen or
health food shop)

TO FINISH

100g granulated sugar

A few drops carmine
red food colouring

or

Edible ruby glitter (see
page 205)

of the oven, slide the shells on to the work surface.

For the lychee and rose ganache. Drain the lychees. Blend then strain them to obtain a fine purée. You will need 240g purée.

Chop up the chocolate and melt it in a bowl over a pan of barely simmering water.

Bring the cream and lychee purée to the boil. Pour it over the melted chocolate a third at a time. Add the rose essence and stir.

Pour the ganache into a gratin dish and press clingfilm over the surface of the ganache. Set aside in the fridge for the ganache to thicken.

Spoon the ganache into a piping bag fitted with a plain nozzle. Pipe a mound of ganache on to half the shells. Lightly press a square of frozen jelly into the centre and finish with a dot of ganache. Top with the remaining shells.

Store the macarons for 24 hours in the fridge and bring back out at the point of serving.

THE STARTING POINT FOR THIS MACARON WAS A CAKE CALLED 'PARADIS' ('PARADISE'), WHICH I CREATED IN 1987, BASED ON THE ASSOCIATION OF ROSE AND RASPBERRY. OVER TIME, I CAME TO REALISE THAT LYCHEES HAVE A ROSE FLAVOUR. WHEN I ADDED JUICY, TANGY RASPBERRIES TO THE ROSE CREAM AND TENDER MACARON, I CAME UP WITH THE ISPAHAN IN 1997.

INFINITELY VANILLA MACARON

Vanilla from Mexico, Madagascar and Tahiti

TO MY MIND, NO ONE VANILLA IS BETTER THAN ANOTHER, BUT I WANTED TO CREATE A 'HOUSE' VANILLA FLAVOUR TO CAPTURE MY IDEA OF VANILLA: WOODY AND FLORAL WITH UNDERTONES OF ALMOND. I TESTED THE VANILLAS OF LAURENCE CAILLER AND CHOSE TO COMBINE VANILLAS FROM TAHITI, MEXICO AND MADAGASCAR.

Makes about 72 macarons (or about 144 shells)

PREPARATION TIME:

about 1 hour

COOKING TIME:

about 25 minutes

STANDING TIME:

30 minutes

REFRIGERATION:

24 hours

INFUSION:

30 minutes

FOR THE MACARON SHELLS

300g ground almonds

300g icing sugar

110g 'liquefied' egg whites (see page 11)

3 vanilla pods

+

300g caster sugar

75g mineral water

110g 'liquefied' egg whites (see page 11)

FOR THE VANILLA GANACHE

400g liquid crème fraîche or whipping cream (35% fat)

2 Mexican vanilla pods

2 Madagascan vanilla pods

2 Tahitian vanilla pods

440g Valrhona Ivoire couverture or white chocolate

Sift together the icing sugar and ground almonds. Split the vanilla pods in two. Scrape out the seeds with the blade of a knife and add them to the mixture of icing sugar and ground almonds. Pour over them the first portion of liquefied egg whites, but do not stir.

Bring the water and sugar to boil at 118°C. When the syrup reaches 115°C, simultaneously start whisking the second portion of liquefied egg whites to soft peaks.

When the sugar reaches 118°C, pour it over the egg whites. Whisk and allow the meringue to cool down to 50°C, then fold it into the almond-sugar mixture. Spoon the batter into a piping bag fitted with a plain nozzle.

Pipe rounds of batter 3.5 cm in diameter, spacing them 2 cm apart on baking trays lined with baking parchment. Rap the baking trays on the work surface covered with a kitchen cloth. Leave the shells to stand for at least 30 minutes until they form a skin.

Preheat the fan oven to 180°C then put the trays in the oven. Bake for 12 minutes quickly opening and shutting the oven door twice during cooking time. Out of the oven, slide the shells on to the work surface.

For the vanilla ganache. Split the vanilla pods in two and scrape out the seeds with the blade of a knife. Stir them into the liquid crème fraîche or whipping cream (35% fat) with the scraped out vanilla pods.

Bring the cream to the boil. Take off the heat, cover and leave to infuse for 30 minutes.

Chop up the chocolate and melt it in a bowl over a pan of barely simmering water. Remove the vanilla pods from the cream and wiping them off one at a time. Pour the cream over the melted chocolate a third at a time. Transfer it to a gratin dish and allow to cool.

Spoon the ganache into a piping bag with a plain nozzle. Pipe a generous mound of ganache on to half the shells. Top with the remaining shells.

Store the macarons for 24 hours in the fridge and bring back out two hours before serving.

To flavour the macaron batter with vanilla, rub the vanilla seeds into the mixture of icing sugar and ground almonds between your hands.

MOGADOR MACARON

Milk chocolate and passion fruit

Makes about 72 macarons (or about 144 shells)

PREPARATION TIME:

about 1 hour

COOKING TIME:

about 25 minutes

STANDING TIME:

30 minutes

REFRIGERATION:

2 hours + 24 hours

FOR THE MACARON SHELLS

300g ground almonds

300g icing sugar

110g 'liquefied' egg whites (see page 11)

5g approx. lemon yellow food colouring

½ g approx. red food colouring (½ coffee spoon)

+

300g caster sugar

75g mineral water

110g 'liquefied' egg whites (see page 11)

FOR THE PASSION FRUIT AND MILK CHOCOLATE GANACHE

100g 'La Viette' butter (sweet butter from Charentes) at room temperature

Sift together the icing sugar and ground almonds.

Stir the food colouring into the first portion of liquefied egg whites. Pour them over the mixture of icing sugar and ground almonds but do not stir.

Bring the water and sugar to boil at 118°C. When the syrup reaches 115°C, simultaneously start whisking the second portion of liquefied egg whites to soft peaks.

When the sugar reaches 118°C, pour it over the egg whites. Whisk and allow the meringue to cool down to 50°C, then fold it into the ground almond-icing sugar mixture. Spoon the batter into a piping bag fitted with a plain nozzle.

Pipe rounds of batter about 3.5 cm in diameter, spacing them 2 cm apart on baking trays lined with baking parchment. Rap the baking trays on the work surface covered with a kitchen cloth. Using a sieve, sprinkle the shells with a light dusting of cocoa powder. Leave the shells to stand for at least 30 minutes until they form a skin.

Preheat the fan oven to 180°C then put the trays in the oven. Bake for 12 minutes quickly opening and shutting the oven door twice during cooking time. Out of the oven, slide the shells on to the work surface.

For the ganache. Cut the butter into pieces. Chop up the chocolate with a serrated knife.

Halve the passion fruit and scoop out the seeds with a teaspoon. Strain the fruit to obtain 250g juice. Weigh the juice and bring it to the boil.

Partially melt the chopped chocolate in a bowl over a pan of barely simmering water. Pour the hot juice over the chocolate a third at a time.

When the temperature of the mixture reaches 60°C, add the pieces of

MILK CHOCOLATE BRINGS OUT EVERY ASPECT OF PASSION FRUIT: ITS FRAGRANCE AND ITS SUBTLE, TANGY SWEETNESS. THE DIFFERENT FLAVOURS BLEND TO CREATE A VIBRANT HARMONY AND COMPLEMENT ONE ANOTHER.

550g Valrhona Jivara chocolate or milk chocolate, 40% cocoa solids

10 passion fruits (for 250g juice)

TO FINISH

Cocoa powder

Make sure you weigh out 250g of juice when you strain the fresh passion fruit. You can sometimes find frozen passion fruit juice in delicatessens. Check that it contains no more than 5% sugar.

butter a few at a time. Stir to obtain a smooth ganache.

Pour the ganache into a gratin dish and press clingfilm over the surface of the ganache. Set aside in the fridge for the ganache to thicken.

Spoon the ganache into a piping bag fitted with a plain nozzle. Pipe a generous mound of ganache on to half the shells. Top with the remaining shells.

Store the macarons for 24 hours in the fridge and bring back out 2 hours before serving.

MONTEBELLO MACARON

Pistachio and raspberry

Makes about 72 macarons
  (or about 144 shells)

PREPARATION TIME:

about 1 hour 30 minutes

COOKING TIME:

about 35 minutes

STANDING TIME:

30 minutes

REFRIGERATION:

2 hours + 24 hours

FOR THE RASPBERRY JELLY

300g fresh or frozen
  raspberries

60g caster sugar

2 gelatine leaves (2g each)

FOR THE PISTACHIO
MACARON SHELLS

150g ground almonds

150g icing sugar

55g 'liquefied' egg whites
  (see page 11)

1g lemon yellow food
  colouring

2g pistachio green food
  colouring

+

150g caster sugar

38g mineral water

55g 'liquefied' egg whites
  (see page 11)

You can also make these macarons using a single batter for the shells.

Start by preparing the raspberry jelly. Soak the gelatine leaves for 15 minutes in cold water to soften. Blend the raspberries with the sugar using a hand blender. Strain the purée to remove the pips. Heat a quarter of the purée to 45°C. Drain and dry the gelatine and add it to the hot purée. Stir, then add the rest of the raspberry purée. Pour into a gratin dish lined with clingfilm to a depth of 4 mm. Leave to cool for 1 hour at room temperature then put the dish in the freezer for 2 hours. Turn out the jelly and cut it into 1.5 cm squares. Return the squares of jelly to the freezer.

For the pistachio macaron shells. Sift together the icing sugar and ground almonds. Stir the food colouring into the first portion of liquefied egg whites. Pour them over the mixture of icing sugar and ground almonds but do not stir.

Bring the water and sugar to boil at 118°C. When the syrup reaches 115°C, simultaneously start whisking the second portion of liquefied egg whites to soft peaks. When the sugar reaches 118°C, pour it over the egg whites. Whisk and allow the meringue to cool to 50°C, then fold it into the almond-icing sugar mixture. Spoon the batter into a piping bag fitted with a plain nozzle.

Pipe rounds of batter about 3.5 cm in diameter, spacing them 2 cm apart on baking trays lined with parchment. Rap the baking trays on the work surface covered with a kitchen cloth. Leave the shells to stand for at least 30 minutes until they form a skin.

For the red macaron shells. Sift together the icing sugar and ground almonds. Stir the food colouring into the first portion of liquefied egg whites. Pour them over the mixture of icing sugar and ground almonds but do not stir. Bring the water and sugar to boil at 118°C. When the syrup reaches 115°C, simultaneously start whisking the second portion of liquefied egg whites to soft peaks.

When the sugar reaches 118°C, pour it over the egg whites. Whisk and allow the meringue to cool down to 50°C, then fold it into the almond-icing sugar mixture. Spoon the batter into a piping bag fitted with a plain nozzle.

150g ground almonds

150g icing sugar

55g 'liquefied' egg
   whites (see page 11)

11g raspberry red food
   colouring

+

150g caster sugar

38g mineral water

55g 'liquefied' egg
   whites (see page 11)

225g liquid crème
   fraîche or whipping
   cream (35% fat)
   with 32-34% fat

225g Valrhona Ivoire
   couverture or white
   chocolate

35g pure pistachio
   paste (or 35g shelled
   unsalted pistachios
   blended with the
   cream)

Pipe rounds of batter 3.5 cm in diameter, spacing them 2 cm apart on baking trays lined with parchment. Rap the baking trays on the work surface covered with a kitchen cloth. Leave the shells to stand for at least 30 minutes until they form a skin.

Preheat the fan oven to 180°C then put the trays in the oven. Bake for 12 minutes quickly opening and shutting the oven door twice during cooking time. Out of the oven, slide the shells on to the work surface.

For the pistachio ganache. Chop up the chocolate and melt it in a bowl over a pan of barely simmering water. Bring the cream to the boil with the pistachio paste. Pour it over the chocolate a third at a time. Stir to obtain a smooth ganache.

Transfer it to a gratin dish. Press clingfilm over the surface of the ganache. Set aside in the fridge for the ganache to thicken. Pour the ganache into a piping bag fitted with a plain nozzle.

Pipe a generous mound of pistachio ganache on to the shells. Lightly press a cube of frozen jelly into the centre. Pipe a dot of ganache on top then cover with the remaining shells.

Store the macarons in the fridge for 24 hours and bring them back out 2 hours before serving.

IN 1985, AS AN ALTERNATIVE TO THE CLASSIC STRAWBERRY TART AND NO LESS TRADITIONAL STRAWBERRY SPONGE, I CAME UP WITH THE IDEA FOR THE MONTEBELLO CAKE THAT MARRIED STRAWBERRIES AND PISTACHIO IN THE FORM OF A CREAM AND DACQUOISE BISCUIT.

FOR THE MACARON, I ADD EITHER A SQUARE OF RASPBERRY JELLY OR A SQUARE OF STRAW-BERRY JELLY TO THE GANACHE – BOTH COMBINATIONS ARE DIVINE.

SARAH MACARON
Chestnuts and Matcha green tea

Makes about 72 macarons (or
   about 144 shells)

PREPARATION TIME:

the day before, 20 minutes;
   next day, 1 hour

COOKING TIME:

about 35 minutes

STANDING TIME:

30 minutes

REFRIGERATION:

2 hours + 24 hours

FOR THE MATCHA GREEN
TEA GANACHE

125g Valrhona Ivoire
   couverture or white
   chocolate

125g liquid crème fraîche or
   whipping cream (35% fat)

10g Matcha green tea

FOR THE PISTACHIO
MACARON SHELLS

300g ground almonds

300g icing sugar

115g 'liquefied' egg whites
   (see page 11)

60g cacao pâte (or dark
   chocolate, 100% cocoa
   solids)

6g Trablit coffee extract

The day before, prepare the Matcha green tea ganache. Chop up the chocolate and melt it in a bowl over a pan of barely simmering water.

Bring the cream to the boil. Allow to cool to 60°C. Add the Matcha tea and whisk briskly by hand. Pour the flavoured hot cream over the chocolate a third at a time.

Pour the ganache into a gratin dish lined with clingfilm to a depth of 4 mm. Set aside in the fridge to cool for 1 hour then transfer the dish to the freezer for 2 hours.

Turn out the ganache and cut it into 1.5 cm squares. Return the squares to the freezer.

Next day, prepare the chestnut purée. Sift together the icing sugar and ground almonds.

Melt the cacao pâte at 50°C in a bowl over a pan of barely simmering water. Stir the colouring and coffee extract into the first portion of liquefied egg whites. Add them to the mixture of icing sugar and ground almonds but do not stir.

Bring the water and sugar to the boil at 118°C. When the syrup reaches 115°C, simultaneously start whisking the second portion of liquefied egg whites to soft peaks.

When the sugar reaches 118°C, pour it over the egg whites. Whisk and allow the meringue to cool down to 50°C, add it to the almond-icing sugar mixture and stir, then fold in the melted cacao. Spoon the batter into a piping bag fitted with a plain nozzle.

DURING MY MANY TRIPS TO JAPAN, I TASTED DIFFERENT KINDS OF MATCHA GREEN TEA AND I NOTICED THAT SOME OF THEM HAD A CHESTNUTTY FLAVOUR. I WANTED TO BRING OUT THIS QUALITY IN A COMBINATION OF PERFECTLY BALANCED FLAVOURS. 'SARAH' IS A PAIRING OF FLAVOURS THAT HAS BECOME ONE OF THE FETISH FLAVOURS OF PIERRE HERMÉ, PARIS. I ALSO ADD PASSION FRUIT, BUT I DELIBERATELY LEFT IT OUT OF THIS MACARON.

2g carmine red food
   colouring

+

300g caster sugar

75g mineral water

115g 'liquefied' egg
   whites (see page 11)

FOR THE MARRON
GLACÉS CREAM

190g marrons glacés
   crumbs (or crushed
   whole marrons
   glacés)

230g 'La Viette' butter
   (sweet butter from
   Charentes) at room
   temperature

235g chestnut purée

155g chestnut paste

15g old brown JM
   Agricole rum

TO FINISH

Matcha green tea

or

Edible 'bronze glitter'
   (see page 205)

You need to rinse the marrons glacés crumbs in warm water to wash off as much of the sugar coating as possible.

Pipe rounds of batter about 3.5 cm in diameter, spacing them 2 cm apart on baking trays lined with baking parchment. Rap the trays on the work surface covered with a kitchen cloth. Using a sieve, sprinkle the shells with a light dusting of Matcha green tea or edible bronze glitter. Leave the shells to stand for at least 30 minutes until they form a skin.

Preheat the fan oven to 180°C then put the trays in the oven. Bake for 12 minutes quickly opening and shutting the oven door twice during cooking time. Out of the oven, slide the shells on to the work surface.

For the marrons glacés cream. Rinse the marrons glacés crumbs in warm water. Drain and dry them then chop them finely.

Crumble the chestnut paste into the rum with the chestnut purée. Beat in the electric mixer fitted with the paddle attachment, then remove the mixture obtained.

In the bowl of the mixer fitted with the paddle attachment, beat the butter to a creamy consistency. Add the chestnut and rum mixture. Beat for a further 8 minutes. Add the marrons glacés crumbs. Stir for a few seconds. Spoon the marrons glacés cream straight into a piping bag fitted with a plain nozzle.

Pipe a generous mound of cream on to half the shells. Lightly press a square of Matcha green tea ganache into the centre. Pipe another dot of ganache on top, then cover with the remaining shells.

Store the macarons in the fridge for 24 hours and bring them back out 2 hours before serving.

PLENITUDE MACARON
Chocolate and caramel

Makes about 72 macarons
(or about 144 shells)

PREPARATION TIME:
about 1 hour 30 minutes

COOKING TIME:
about 35 minutes

STANDING TIME:
30 minutes

REFRIGERATION:
3 hours + 24 hours

FOR THE FLEUR DE SEL
CHOCOLATE CHIPS

100g Valrhona Guanaja
chocolate or dark
chocolate, 70% cocoa
solids

2g fleur de sel

FOR THE CHOCOLATE
MACARON SHELLS

60g cacao pâte or dark
chocolate, 100% cocoa
solids

150g ground almonds

150g icing sugar

55g 'liquefied' egg whites
(see page 11)

2g carmine red food
colouring

+

165g caster sugar

38g mineral water

55g 'liquefied' egg whites
(see page 11)

Start by preparing the fleur de sel chocolate chips. Crush the fleur de sel using a rolling pin.

Chop up the chocolate with a serrated knife then melt it in a bowl over a saucepan of barely simmering water. Stir the crushed fleur de sel into the chocolate. Pour the chocolate on to a piece of plastic, such as a plastic divider. Spread the chocolate into a fine layer using a spatula then cover with a second piece of plastic and lay a weight over the whole surface so that the chocolate holds its shape. Set aside in the fridge for 3 hours. Break it up into little chocolate chips. Set aside in the fridge. It is best to temper the chocolate but you do not have to for this recipe as the chips will not be visible.

For the chocolate macaron shells. Sift together the icing sugar and ground almonds. Melt the cacao pâte at 50°C in a bowl over a pan of barely simmering water. Stir the food colouring into the first portion of liquefied egg whites. Add them to the mixture of icing sugar and ground almonds but do not stir.

Bring the water and sugar to the boil at 118°C. When the syrup reaches 115°C, simultaneously start whisking the second portion of liquefied egg whites to soft peaks. When the sugar reaches 118°C, pour it over the egg whites. Whisk and allow the meringue to cool down to 50°C, then fold it into the almond-icing sugar mixture. Spoon the batter into a piping bag fitted with a plain nozzle.

Pipe rounds of batter about 3.5 cm in diameter, spacing them 2 cm apart on baking trays lined with baking parchment. Rap the trays on the work surface covered with a kitchen cloth. Using a sieve, sprinkle the shells with a light dusting of cocoa powder. Leave the shells to stand for at least 30 minutes until they form a skin.

For the caramel shells. Sift together the icing sugar and ground almonds. Stir the coffee extract

You can also use a single batter for the macaron shells.

I like to push the caramelisation of the sugar to its limits to obtain an intense caramel flavour that is not too bitter.

CHOCOLATE AND CARAMEL IS A CLASSIC COMBINATION. MY INTERPRETATION WAS INSPIRED BY A VISIT TO A SWEDISH CONFECTIONER'S CALLED 'DAIM'. I ADD A COUNTERPOINT OF CRISP DARK CHOCOLATE CHIPS WITH FLEUR DE SEL TO THE SWEET CARAMEL FLAVOUR.

150g ground almonds

150g icing sugar

55g 'liquefied' egg
whites (see page 11)

7g Trablit coffee
extract

7g egg yellow food
colouring

+

150g caster sugar

38g mineral water

55g 'liquefied' egg
whites (see page 11)

110g caster sugar

20g lightly salted 'La
Viette' butter (sweet
butter from
Charentes) at room
temperature

250g liquid crème
fraîche or whipping
cream (35% fat)

250g Valrhona
Caribbean
couverture or 64%
dark chocolate

125g Valrhona Jivara
couverture or 40%
dark chocolate

Cocoa powder

into the first portion of liquefied egg whites. Add the mixture of icing sugar and ground almonds but do not stir.

Bring the water and sugar to the boil at 118°C. When the syrup reaches 115°C, simultaneously start whisking the second portion of liquefied egg whites to soft peaks.

When the sugar reaches 118°C, pour it over the egg whites. Whisk and allow the meringue to cool down to 50°C, then fold it into the almond-icing sugar mixture. Spoon the batter into a piping bag fitted with a plain nozzle.

Pipe rounds of batter about 3.5 cm in diameter, spacing them 2 cm apart on baking trays lined with baking parchment.

Rap the trays on the work surface covered with a kitchen cloth.

Using a sieve, sprinkle the shells with a light dusting of cocoa powder.

Leave the shells to stand for at least 30 minutes until they form a skin.

Preheat the fan oven to 180°C then put the trays into the oven. Bake for 12 minutes quickly opening and shutting the oven door twice during cooking time.

Out of the oven, slide the shells on to the work surface.

For the chocolate and caramel ganache. Chop up all the chocolate and melt it in a bowl over a pan of barely simmering water.

Bring the cream to the boil. Put 50g of the sugar into a large saucepan. Heat it till it melts then add the rest of the sugar. Allow the sugar to caramelise and turn a deep amber colour.

Take the saucepan off the heat. Add the lightly salted butter, taking care as it may bubble and spit. Stir, then pour in the hot cream and stir. Pour it over the melted chocolate a third at a time.

Pour into a gratin dish. Press clingfilm over the surface of the ganache and set aside in the fridge for it to thicken.

Spoon the ganache into a piping bag fitted with a plain nozzle.
Pipe a generous mound of ganache on to half the shells. Sprinkle with 3 or 4 fleur de sel dark chocolate chips. Top them with the remaining shells.

Store the macarons in the fridge for 24 hours. Remove from the fridge two hours before eating.

MOSAIC MACARON

*Pistachio and cinnamon ganache with Griottines® cherries
(Morello cherries macerated in Kirsch)*

Makes about 72 macarons
  (or about 144 shells)

PREPARATION TIME:

about 1 hour 15 minutes

COOKING TIME:

about 55 minutes

STANDING TIME:

30 minutes

REFRIGERATION:

2 hours + 24 hours

FOR THE MACARON SHELLS

300g ground almonds

300g icing sugar

110g 'liquefied' egg whites
  (see page 11)

+

300g caster sugar

75g mineral water

110g 'liquefied' egg whites
  (see page 11)

FOR THE PISTACHIO AND
CINNAMON GANACHE WITH
GRIOTTINES® CHERRIES

375g liquid crème fraîche or
  whipping cream (35% fat)

10g Ceylon cinnamon sticks

375g Valrhona Ivoire
  couverture or white
  chocolate

55g pistachio paste (or 55g
  unsalted shelled pistachios
  blended with the cream)

150g pitted Griottines®

For the coloured sugar. Preheat the oven to 60°C.

Stir a few drops of food colouring into the sugar, then, wearing disposable gloves, rub the mixture between the palms of your hands. Spread out the coloured sugar on a baking tray. Put it in the oven and dry it for 30 minutes.

Sift together the icing sugar and ground almonds then tip the dry mixture into the first portion of liquefied eggs but do not stir.

Bring the water and sugar to the boil at 118°C. When the syrup reaches 115°C, simultaneously start whisking the second portion of liquefied egg whites to soft peaks.

When the sugar reaches 118°C, pour it over the egg whites. Whisk and allow the meringue to cool down to 50°C, then fold it into the almond-icing sugar mixture. Spoon the batter into a piping bag fitted with a plain nozzle.

Pipe rounds of batter about 3.5 cm in diameter, spacing them 2 cm apart on baking trays lined with parchment.

Rap the baking trays on the work surface covered with a kitchen cloth.

Sprinkle every other row with pinches of coloured sugar (or with ruby glitter).

Leave the shells to stand for at least 30 minutes until they form a skin.

Preheat the fan oven to 180°C then put the trays in the oven. Bake for 12 minutes quickly opening and shutting the oven door twice during cooking time.

Out of the oven, slide the shells on to the work surface.

For the pistachio ganache. Chop up the chocolate then melt it in a bowl over a pan of barely simmering water. Bring the cream to the boil with the cinnamon. Take the cream off the heat. Allow to infuse for 4 minutes then strain the cream. Stir in the pistachio paste, then pour the hot infused cream over the melted chocolate a third at a time. Blend the cream with a hand blender.

100g granulated sugar

A few drops of red
food colouring

or

Edible ruby glitter (see
page 205)

Transfer to a gratin dish. Press clingfilm over the surface of the ganache. Set aside in the fridge for the ganache to thicken.

Spoon the ganache into a piping bag fitted with a plain nozzle.

Drain the Griottines® cherries. Pipe a generous mound of ganache on to half the shells. Lightly press a Griottine® cherry into the centre and top with the remaining shells.

Store the macarons in the fridge for 24 hours and bring them back out 2 hours before serving.

I DEVELOPED A MACARON WITH GRIOTTINES® CHERRIES, PISTACHIO AND CEYLON CINNAMON AT THE REQUEST OF MR BAUD OF DISTILLERIES PEREUX. THE FIRST CONFECTION THAT MARRIED PISTACHIO WITH CHERRIES, IN 1983, WAS CALLED 'ARLEQUIN' ('HARLEQUIN'). LATER, I CREATED VARIATIONS, LIKE THE CRISP TART WITH CHERRIES AND PISTACHIO OR 'MOSAIC EMOTION' AND MOSAIC FRUIT JELLIES…

SATINE MACARON

Passion fruit, orange and cream cheese

Makes about 72 macarons (or about 144 shells)

PREPARATION TIME:

about 1 hour 30 minutes

COOKING TIME:

about 35 minutes

STANDING TIME:

2 x 30 minutes

REFRIGERATION:

24 hours

FOR THE ORANGE AND PASSION FRUIT JELLY

7 passion fruits (for 15g juice)

85g top-quality orange marmalade

120g mineral water

10g caster sugar

3 gelatine leaves (2g each)

FOR THE WHITE MACARON SHELLS

150g ground almonds

150g icing sugar

55g 'liquefied' egg whites (see page 11)

7.5g titanium oxide powder + 5g warm mineral water

+

150g caster sugar

38g mineral water

55g 'liquefied' egg whites (see page 11)

Start by making the orange and passion fruit jelly. Soak the gelatine leaves for 15 minutes in cold water to soften.

Halve the passion fruits and scrape out the seeds. Strain the flesh to obtain 150g juice. Bring the passion fruit juice to the boil with the orange marmalade, sugar and water, stirring constantly. Add the drained gelatine and stir. Pour into a gratin dish lined with clingfilm to a depth of 4 mm. Set aside in the fridge for 1 hour then transfer the dish to the freezer for 2 hours.

Turn out the jelly and cut it into 1.5 cm squares. Return the jelly squares to the freezer.

For the white macaron shells. Sift together the icing sugar and ground almonds.

Dilute the titanium oxide powder in the warm mineral water then stir it into the first portion of liquefied egg whites. Pour it over the mixture of icing sugar and ground almonds but do not stir.

Bring the water and sugar to the boil at 118°C. When the syrup reaches 115°C, simultaneously start whisking the second portion of liquefied egg whites to soft peaks.

When the sugar reaches 118°C, pour it over the egg whites. Whisk and allow the meringue to cool down to 50°C, then fold it into the almond-icing sugar mixture. Spoon the batter into a piping bag fitted with a plain nozzle.

Pipe rounds of batter about 3.5 cm in diameter, spacing them 2 cm apart on baking trays lined with parchment.

Rap the baking trays on the work surface covered with a kitchen cloth.

Leave the shells to stand for about 30 minutes until a skin forms on the surface.

For the yellow macaron shells. Sift together the icing sugar and ground almonds.

Stir the food colouring into the first portion of liquefied egg whites. Pour it over the mixture of icing sugar and ground almonds but do not stir.

Bring the water and sugar to the boil at 118°C. When the syrup reaches 115°C, simultaneously start whisking the second

You can also make these macarons using a single batter, either white or yellow, as you prefer.

FOR THE YELLOW
MACARON SHELLS

150g ground almonds

150g icing sugar

55g 'liquefied' egg whites
    (see page 11)

2.5g approx. lemon
    yellow food colouring

A few drops carmine red
    food colouring

+

150g caster sugar

38g mineral water

55g 'liquefied' egg whites
    (see page 11)

FOR THE CREAM CHEESE
BUTTER CREAM

100g caster sugar

30g mineral water

75g whole eggs

45g egg yolk

165g very soft butter

375g Philadelphia cream
    cheese

portion of liquefied egg whites to soft peaks.

When the sugar reaches 118°C, pour it over the egg whites. Whisk and allow the meringue to cool to 50°C, then fold it into the mixture of almond-icing sugar mixture. Spoon the batter into a piping bag fitted with a plain nozzle.

Pipe rounds of batter about 3.5 cm in diameter, spacing them 2 cm apart on baking trays lined with baking parchment. Rap the trays on the work surface covered with a kitchen cloth. Leave the shells to stand for at least 30 minutes until a skin forms on the surface.

Preheat the fan oven to 180°C then put the trays of white shells and yellow shells in the oven. Bake for 12 minutes quickly opening and shutting the oven door twice during cooking time. Out of the oven, slide the shells on to the work surface.

For the cream-cheese cream. In a saucepan, bring the sugar and water to the boil. When it boils, clean the sides of the pan with a damp pastry brush. Heat the sugar syrup to 120°C.

In a bowl, whisk the eggs and yolks until they lighten in colour. Pour in the hot sugar at 120°C and continue whisking until completely cool.

In the bowl of an electric mixer, whisk the butter until it thickens. Add the egg mixture and continue whisking to obtain a smooth cream.

Weigh out 250g butter cream and whisk with the cream cheese. Spoon the cream into a piping bag with a plain nozzle. Pipe mounds of cream on to the white shells. Gently press a fruit jelly square into the centre and dot each one with a little cream. Top them with the remaining Satine shells.

Store the macarons in the fridge for 24 hours and bring back out immediately before eating.

I WANTED TO TRANSPOSE THE FLAVOUR OF PHILADELPHIA CREAM CHEESE TO THE SOFT, MELTING CONSISTENCY OF A MACARON AND ADD THE SWEET, ZESTY FLAVOURS OF ORANGE AND PASSION FRUIT. THIS MARRIAGE OF FLAVOURS IS NAMED AFTER A FAMOUS MOULIN-ROUGE CABARET DANCER CALLED SATINE.

SIGNATURE
MACARONS

'MY MACARONS COMPOSED OVER THE YEARS AND MY PREFERENCES WHICH HAVE BECOME MY SIGNATURES.'

OLIVE OIL AND VANILLA MACARON

Makes about 72 macarons (or about 144 shells)

PREPARATION TIME:

about 1 hour

COOKING TIME:

about 25 minutes

STANDING TIME:

30 minutes

REFRIGERATION:

24 hours

FOR THE MACARON SHELLS

300g ground almonds

300g icing sugar

110g 'liquefied' egg whites (see page 11)

+

300g caster sugar

75g mineral water

110g 'liquefied' egg whites (see page 11)

10g Trablit coffee extract

1.5g approx. green food colouring

Sift together the icing sugar and ground almonds. Stir the food colouring into the first portion of fresh egg whites. Pour them over the mixture of icing sugar and ground almonds but do not stir.

Bring the water and sugar to the boil at 118°C. When the syrup reaches 115°C, simultaneously start whisking the second portion of liquefied egg whites to soft peaks. When the sugar reaches 118°C, pour it over the egg whites. Whisk and allow the meringue to cool down to 50°C, then fold it into the almond-sugar mixture. Spoon the batter into a piping bag with a plain nozzle.

Pipe rounds of batter about 3.5 cm in diameter, spacing them 2 cm apart on baking trays lined with baking parchment. Rap the trays on the work surface covered with a kitchen cloth. Leave to stand for at least 30 minutes until a skin forms on the shells.

Preheat the fan oven to 180°C then put the trays in the oven. Bake for 12 minutes quickly opening and shutting the oven door twice during cooking time. Out of the oven, slide the shells on to the work surface.

For the olive oil ganache. Rinse the olives several times in cold water. Drain and carefully dry them. Halve them and remove the stone, cut them into little cubes about 2 mm in size then set aside in the fridge. (Cont.)

IN 1994 IN ITALY, I TRIED A FRUIT CAKE MADE WITH OLIVE OIL. ITS TASTE AND UNIQUE TEXTURE MADE SUCH A PROFOUND IMPRESSION ON ME THAT IT OPENED UP A WHOLE NEW RAFT OF POSSIBILITIES TO ME. WITH OLIVER BAUSSAN, A GREAT CONNOISSEUR AND A BIG PROPONENT OF OLIVE OIL THROUGHOUT THE WORLD, I HAD ALSO SAMPLED THE 'LATIUM', A SUPERB ITALIAN OIL WITH A SWEE-TISH FLAVOUR AND ACCENTS OF VANILLA. I USED IT IN AN OLIVE OIL AND VANILLA SORBET, THEN IN MY PASTRIES. IT SEEMED AN OBVIOUS MOVE TO INCLUDE IT IN MY MACARONS. THE FRUIT FLAVOUR AND SPICY, DELICATE FRESHNESS COMBINED WITH MADAGASCAR VANILLA GIVE THE MACARON ITS UNIQUE CHARACTER.

FOR THE OLIVE OIL
AND VANILLA
GANACHE

350g Valrhona Ivoire
couverture or white
chocolate

150g liquid crème
fraîche or whipping
cream (35% fat)
with 32/34% fat

½ vanilla pod

225g Laurent Tellier
100% first press
olive oil, Aglando
variety (see page
205)

30 Lucques green
olives in brine

Don't stir the pieces of
green olive into the
ganache as this will make
the ganache too salty.
Simply lay them on the
ganache before topping
with the remaining shells.
High quality olive oil is
essential, preferably from a
producer rather than a
mass-market brand.

Chop up the chocolate and melt it in a bowl over a pan of barely simmering water. Place half a split vanilla pod with the seeds scraped out in the cream and bring to the boil.

Take out the vanilla pod then pour the cream over the melted chocolate. Stir, then drizzle in the olive oil at room temperature and use a hand blender to blend to a smooth ganache. Transfer to a gratin dish and allow to stand at room temperature until it starts to grow firm.

Pour the ganache into a piping bag with a plain nozzle. Pipe a generous mound of ganache on to half the shells. Press 3 pieces of green olives into each filled macaron. Top with the remaining shells.

Store the macarons for 24 hours in the fridge and bring back out two hours before serving.

GRAPEFRUIT AMERICANO MACARON

Grapefruit, orange and Campari

Makes about 72
  macarons (or about
  144 shells)

PREPARATION TIME:

the day before, 15
  minutes; next day,
  about 1 hour

COOKING TIME:

about 1 hour 50 minutes

STANDING TIME:

30 minutes

REFRIGERATION:

2 hours + 24 hours

FOR THE CANDIED
GRAPEFRUIT

2 untreated grapefruit

1 litre water

500g caster sugar

1 star anise

10g Sarawak black
  peppercorns

1 vanilla pod

4 tablespoons lemon
  juice

FOR THE MACARON
SHELLS

300g ground almonds

300g icing sugar

110g 'liquefied' egg
  whites (see page 11)

3g carmine red food
  colouring

Make sure you don't boil the citrus and Campari juice because that would spoil the flavour. Use an electronic thermometer to take the temperature of the juice, which should not be more than 45°C.

Don't stir the grapefruit cubes into the ganache, as you will end up with a uniformly bitter cream. By placing the pieces of candied grapefruit on the cream, you create layers of flavour.

The day before, wash and dry the grapefruits. Cut off both ends. Using a knife, cut thick segments from top to bottom and trim off the peel and a good centimetre of flesh. Immerse the zests obtained in a pan of boiling water. Bring the water back to the boil and cook for 2 minutes then drain. Refresh in cold water. Repeat this step twice more. Drain the zests.

Grind the peppercorns. Put them in a saucepan with the water, sugar and lemon juice, the star anise and the split vanilla pod with the seeds scraped out. Bring to the boil over a low heat. Add the zests. Put a lid on the pan so that it three-quarters covers it and simmer very gently for 1 hour 30 minutes. Cover with clingfilm and store in the fridge until next day.

Next day, in a sieve over a bowl, drain the candied grapefruit for an hour. Cut into 3 mm cubes.

For the macaron shells. Sift together the icing sugar and ground almonds. Stir the food colouring into the first portion of liquefied egg whites. Add this to the mixture of icing sugar and ground almonds but do not stir.

Bring the water and sugar to the boil at 118°C. When the syrup reaches 115°C, simultaneously start whisking the second portion of liquefied egg whites to soft peaks. When the sugar reaches 118°C, pour it over the egg whites. Whisk and allow to cool down to 50°C, then fold the meringue into the almond-sugar mixture. Spoon the batter into a piping bag with a plain nozzle.

Pipe rounds of batter about 3.5 cm in diameter, spacing them 2 cm apart on baking trays lined with baking parchment. Rap the trays on the work surface covered with a kitchen cloth. Leave to stand for at least 30 minutes until a skin forms on the shells.

Preheat the fan oven to 180°C then put the trays in the oven. Bake for 12 minutes quickly opening and shutting

5g lemon yellow food
   colouring

3g strawberry red food
   colouring

+

300g caster sugar

75g mineral water

110g 'liquefied' egg whites
   (see page 11)

20g fresh lemon juice

110g fresh grapefruit juice

45g fresh orange juice

50g Campari

420g Valrhona Ivoire
   couverture or white
   chocolate

the oven door twice during cooking time. Out of the oven, slide the shells on to the work surface.

For the grapefruit and Campari ganache. Stir together the freshly squeezed lemon, grapefruit and orange juice with the Campari. Chop up the chocolate and melt it in a bowl over a pan of barely simmering water. Heat the Campari and citrus fruit juice to 45°C. Pour it over the melted chocolate a third at a time. Blend for 4 minutes with a hand blender. Pour the ganache into a gratin dish. Press clingfilm over the surface of the ganache and set aside in the fridge for the ganache to thicken.

Pour the ganache into a piping bag with a plain nozzle. Pipe a generous mound of the ganache on to half the shells. Lightly press 2 or 3 cubes of candied grapefruit into the ganache then top with the remaining shells.

Store in the fridge for 24 hours and bring back out 2 hours before serving.

I REMEMBER SITTING ON THE TERRACE OF FERRAN ADRIA'S HACIENDA BENAZUZA IN SEVILLE SIPPING AN AMERICANO COCKTAIL. THE TASTE WAS OUT OF THIS WORLD AND IT GAVE ME THE IDEA FOR THIS COMBINATION OF FLAVOURS. THIS MACARON OFFERS A PERFECT BALANCE OF SWEET, SOUR AND TANGY.

ENVIE MACARON
Violet and blackcurrant

Makes about 72 macarons
  (or about 144 shells)

PREPARATION TIME:

the day before, 10 minutes;
  next day, about 1 hour

COOKING TIME:

the day before, 35 minutes;
  next day, about 25
  minutes

STANDING TIME:

30 minutes

REFRIGERATION:

2 hours + 24 hours

FOR THE FILLING

200g fresh or frozen
  blackcurrants

200g water

100g caster sugar

FOR THE MACARON SHELLS

300g ground almonds

300g icing sugar

15g titanium oxide powder
  diluted in 10g warm
  mineral water

110g 'liquefied' egg whites
  (see page 11)

100g warm mineral water

+

300g caster sugar

75g mineral water

110g 'liquefied' egg whites
  (see page 11)

The day before, prepare the filling. Bring the water and sugar to the boil. Add the frozen blackcurrants to the boiling syrup. Bring it back to the boil, then drain and place the fruit on a cloth to dry until next day.

Still the day before, prepare the coloured sugar to decorate the macarons. Preheat the oven to 60°C. Stir a few drops of colouring into the sugar, then, wearing disposable gloves, rub the mixture between the palms of your hands. Spread out the coloured sugar on a baking tray and place it in the oven to dry for 30 minutes.

Next day, sift together the icing sugar and ground almonds. Dilute the titanium oxide powder in warm mineral water then stir it into the first portion of liquefied egg whites. Add this to the mixture of icing sugar and ground almonds but do not stir.

Bring the water and sugar to the boil at 118°C. When the syrup reaches 115°C, simultaneously start whisking the second portion of liquefied egg whites to soft peaks. When the sugar reaches 118°C, pour it over the egg whites. Whisk and allow to cool down to 50°C, then fold the meringue into the almond-sugar mixture. Spoon the batter into a piping bag with a plain nozzle.

Pipe rounds of batter about 3.5 cm in diameter, spacing them 2 cm apart on baking trays lined with baking parchment. Rap the trays on the work surface covered with a kitchen cloth. Sprinkle the shells with pinches of coloured sugar. Leave to stand for at least 30 minutes until a skin forms on the shells.

Preheat the fan oven to 180°C then put the trays in the oven. Bake for 12 minutes quickly opening and shutting the oven door twice during

VIOLET-FLAVOURED SWEETS WERE THE INSPIRATION BEHIND THIS MACARON. THE TART FLAVOUR OF BLACKCURRANTS IN SYRUP HARMONISES WITH THE FLORAL SUBTLETY OF VIOLETS.

FOR THE VIOLET GANACHE

- 450g liquid crème fraîche or whipping cream (35% fat)
- 525g Valrhona Ivoire couverture or white chocolate
- 8 drops violet essence

TO FINISH

- 100g granulated sugar
- A few drops of violet food colouring

cooking time. Out of the oven, slide the shells on to the work surface.

For the violet ganache. Chop up the chocolate and melt it in a bowl over a pan of barely simmering water. Bring the cream to boil. Pour it over the chocolate in thirds. Stir in a few drops of violet flavouring.

Spoon the ganache into a piping bag with a plain nozzle. Pipe a generous mound of ganache on to half the shells. Press 3 blackcurrants in syrup into the centre and top with the remaining shells.

Store the macarons for 24 hours in the fridge. Bring them back out two hours before serving.

ARABELLA MACARON

Milk chocolate, ginger, passion fruit, banana and almond

Makes about 72 macarons (or about 144 shells)

PREPARATION TIME:

the day before, 20 minutes; next day, about 1 hour

COOKING TIME:

about 35 minutes

STANDING TIME:

30 minutes

REFRIGERATION:

24 hours

FREEZING TIME:

2 hours

FOR THE MACARON SHELLS

300g ground almonds

300g icing sugar

60g cacao pâte

115g 'liquefied' egg whites (see page 11)

1g approx. carmine red food colouring

7.5g egg yellow food colouring

7.5g Trablit coffee extract

+

300g caster sugar

75g mineral water

115g 'liquefied' egg whites (see page 11)

The day before, prepare the compote. Halve the passion fruit and scrape out the pulp and seeds. Slice the ripe – but not black – bananas into discs about ½ cm thick and sprinkle them with lemon juice.

In a frying pan, heat the butter. When it turns a nutty colour, add the banana slices. Sprinkle with sugar. Brown them over a high heat. Stir in the passion fruit flesh.

Pour the compote into a gratin dish lined with clingfilm to a depth of 4 mm. Smooth the surface with a spatula. Chill it in the fridge for 1 hour then transfer the dish to the freezer for 2 hours. Turn out the jelly and cut it into 1.5 cm squares. Return the squares to the freezer.

Next day, sift together the icing sugar and ground almonds. Melt the cacao pâte at 50°C in a bowl over a pan of barely simmering water. Stir the food colouring into the first portion of liquefied egg whites. Add to the mixture of icing sugar and ground almonds but do not stir.

Bring the water and sugar to the boil at 118°C. When the syrup reaches 115°C, simultaneously start whisking the second portion of liquefied egg whites to soft peaks. When the sugar reaches 118°C, pour it over the egg whites. Whisk and allow to cool down to 50°C, then add the meringue to the almond-sugar mixture, stir, then fold in the melted cacao. Spoon the batter into a piping bag with a plain nozzle.

Pipe rounds of batter about 3.5 cm in diameter, spacing them 2 cm apart on baking trays lined with baking parchment. Rap the trays on the work surface covered with a kitchen cloth. Leave to stand for at least 30 minutes until a skin forms on the shells.

Preheat the fan oven to 180°C then put the trays in the oven. Bake for 12 minutes quickly opening and shutting the oven door twice during cooking time. Out of the oven, slide the shells on to the work surface.

For the milk chocolate ganache. Rinse the preserved ginger in warm water, rubbing it between your fingers to get rid of as much sugar as possible. Drain and dry the ginger then cut the pieces into 3 mm cubes. Chop up the chocolate and put it in a bowl. Bring the cream to the boil.

5g 'La Viette' butter
(sweet butter from
Charentes)

15g caster sugar

250g peeled banana
(weight without the
skin)

10g lemon juice

1 passion fruit

200g liquid crème
fraîche or whipping
cream (35% fat)

220g Valrhona Jivara
couverture or milk
chocolate, 40%
cocoa solids

40g crystallised ginger
(in jars from the
supermarket or from
delicatessens)

Chopped almonds

Pour it over the chocolate a third at a time. Add the cubes of preserved ginger. Transfer the ganache to a gratin dish. Press clingfilm over the surface of the ganache and set aside in the fridge for the ganache to thicken.

Spoon the ganache into a piping bag with a plain nozzle. Put a square of frozen compote on half the macaron shells and pipe a mound of the ganache over them, then top with the remaining shells.

Store the macarons for 24 hours in the fridge. Bring them back out two hours before serving.

WHEN I FIRST PRODUCED THESE MACARONS IN 2001, I ADDED A SQUARE OF FRESH FRUIT COMPOTE TO A LAYER OF GANACHE AND A PIECE OF DRIED FRUIT. I FOLLOWED MY INSTINCT TO CREATE DARING CONTRASTS OF TEXTURES AND SENSATIONS PREVIOUSLY UNKNOWN IN MACARONS.

FRESH MINT MACARON

Makes about 72 macarons
   (or about 144 shells)

PREPARATION TIME:

about 1 hour

COOKING TIME:

about 25 minutes

STANDING TIME:

30 minutes

REFRIGERATION:

2 hours + 24 hours

FOR THE MACARON
SHELLS

300g ground almonds

300g icing sugar

110g 'liquefied' egg whites
   (see page 11)

10g approx. mint green
   food colouring

+

300g caster sugar

75g mineral water

110g 'liquefied' egg whites
   (see page 11)

FOR THE FRESH MINT
GANACHE

300g liquid crème fraîche
   or whipping cream (35%
   fat)

300g Valrhona Ivoire
   couverture or white
   chocolate

15g crème de menthe

12g fresh mint leaves

120g ground almonds

It is important not to cover the mint leaves while they are infusing in the cream and not to infuse them for more than 10 minutes. Otherwise you will lose that cool mint favour in the ganache. Mint leaves taste like dried grass when they have been infused for too long.

Sift together the icing sugar and ground almonds. Stir the food colouring into the first portion of liquefied egg whites. Pour them over the mixture of icing sugar and ground almonds but do not stir.

Bring the water and sugar to the boil at 118°C. When the syrup reaches 115°C, simultaneously start whisking the second portion of liquefied egg whites to soft peaks. When the sugar reaches 118°C, pour it over the egg whites. Whisk and allow to cool down to 50°C, then add the meringue to the almond-sugar mixture and fold in. Spoon the batter into a piping bag with a plain nozzle.

Pipe rounds of batter about 3.5 cm in diameter, spacing them 2 cm apart on baking trays lined with baking parchment. Rap the trays on the work surface covered with a kitchen cloth. Leave to stand for 30 minutes until a skin forms on the shells. Preheat the fan oven to 180°C.

Put the trays in the oven and bake for 12 minutes quickly opening and shutting the oven door twice during cooking time. Out of the oven, slide the shells on to the work surface.

For the mint ganache. Remove the leaves from the stalks, rinse, dry then finely chop the leaves. Bring the cream to the boil and take it off the heat. Add the chopped mint and infuse uncovered for 10 minutes. Strain the cream and retain the chopped mint. Blend it finely in the blender. Chop the chocolate and melt it in a bowl over a pan of barely simmering water. Pour the hot infused cream over the chocolate a third at a time. Add the chopped mint, the crème de menthe and the ground almonds. Stir, then spoon the ganache into a piping bag with a plain nozzle. Pipe a generous mound of the ganache on to half the shells then top with the remaining shells.

Store the macarons for 24 hours in the fridge. Bring them back out two hours before serving.

IN 2001, I WANTED TO ADAPT THE DELICIOUSLY COOL TASTE OF SIROP DE MENTHE TO A MACARON. ALTHOUGH I RARELY BAKE WITH ALCOHOL, THE ADDITION OF CRÈME DE MENTHE GET BRINGS OUT THE FULL FRAGRANCE AND INTENSE FRESH FLAVOUR OF THE MINT LEAVES.

ARABESQUE MACARON

Apricot and pistachio

Makes about 72 macarons
  (or about 144 shells)

PREPARATION TIME:

about 1 hour 30 minutes

COOKING TIME:

about 3 hours 40 minutes

STANDING TIME:

30 minutes

REFRIGERATION:

2 hours + 24 hours

FREEZING TIME:

2 hours

FOR THE MACARON SHELLS

300g ground almonds

300g icing sugar

110g 'liquefied' egg whites
  (see page 11)

2g approx. lemon yellow
  food colouring

1g approx. strawberry red
  food colouring

1g approx. carmine red
  food colouring

+

300g caster sugar

75g mineral water

110g 'liquefied' egg whites
  (see page 11)

Start by preparing the ground pistachios to finish. Preheat the oven to 60°C. Spread the pistachios out on a baking tray and put in the oven to dry for about 3 hours. Out of the oven, leave them to cool before crushing them in the food processor. Sift to obtain a fine powder.

For the crunchy pistachio praline squares. Preheat the oven to 160°C. Spread the pistachios out on a baking tray and put them in the oven. Roast for about 15 minutes. When they are cold, crush the pistachios in a plastic bag. Crumble the Gavotte biscuits in your fingers. Chop up the Ivoire couverture and melt it with the butter in a bowl over a pan of barely simmering water. Stir the almond paste and pistachio paste into the melted mixture. Add the crumbled Gavotte biscuits and crushed pistachios.

Pour into a gratin dish lined with clingfilm to a depth of 4 mm. Smooth the surface. Chill for 1 hour in the fridge then transfer the dish to the freezer. Turn out the praline and cut it into 1.5 cm squares. Return the squares to the freezer.

For the macaron shells. Sift together the icing sugar and ground almonds. Stir the food colouring into the first portion of liquefied egg whites. Pour them over the mixture of icing sugar and ground almonds but do not stir. Bring the water and sugar to the boil at 118°C. When the syrup reaches 115°C, simultaneously start whisking the second portion of liquefied egg whites to soft peaks. When the sugar reaches 118°C, pour it over the egg whites. Whisk and leave the meringue to cool down to 50°C, then fold it into the almond-sugar mixture. Spoon the batter into a piping bag with a plain nozzle.

IN THE COURSE OF MY CREATIVE WORK ON THE MACARON, I HAVE BEEN KEEN TO ADD NEW TEXTURES TO THE SMOOTH AND SUCCULENT, MELTING CONSISTENCY OF THIS LITTLE DELICACY AND EMPHASISE ITS CHARACTER IN NEW WAYS. IN 2002, I ACHIEVED THIS BY ADDING CRUNCHY PISTA-CHIO AND WAFER-THIN 'CRÊPE DENTELLE' GAVOTTE BISCUITS TO THE SMOOTH APRICOT CREAM.

Pipe rounds of batter about 3.5 cm in diameter, spacing them 2 cm apart on baking trays lined with baking parchment. Rap the trays on the work surface covered with a kitchen cloth. Sprinkle the shells with a light dusting of ground pistachio. Leave the shells to stand for at least 30 minutes until they form a skin.

Preheat the fan oven to 180°C then put the trays in the oven. Bake for 12 minutes quickly opening and shutting the oven door twice during cooking time. Out of the oven, slide the shells on to the work surface.

For the apricot cream. Rinse and dry the apricots. Remove the stones. Blend to a purée using a hand blender. Weigh the purée: you should obtain 270g.

Cut the soft apricots into 2 mm cubes. Chop up the chocolate and melt it in a bowl over a pan of barely simmering water. Bring the apricot purée with the lemon juice to the boil. Pour it over the melted chocolate a third at a time. Add the Abricotine then use a hand blender to blend the cream for 5 minutes. Add the dried apricot cubes. Pour the cream into a gratin dish.

You can prepare the ground pistachios and the squares of crunchy pistachio praline several days in advance and store them in the fridge in air-tight containers.

Soft apricots are partially rehydrated and readily available on the dried fruit aisle in supermarkets.

Press clingfilm over the surface of the cream and set aside in the fridge for the cream to thicken. Spoon the cream into a piping bag with a nozzle.

Pipe a generous mound of ganache on to half the shells. Lightly press a square of the frozen crunchy praline into each filled shell then top with the remaining shells.

Store the macarons for 24 hours in the fridge. Bring them back out 2 hours before serving.

LIME AND BASIL MACARON

Makes about 72 macarons
(or about 144 shells)

PREPARATION TIME:

the day before, 20
minutes; next day,
about 1 hour

COOKING TIME:

the day before, 6 minutes;
next day about 25
minutes

STANDING TIME:

30 minutes

REFRIGERATION:

24 hours + 24 hours

FOR THE MACARON
SHELLS

300g ground almonds

300g icing sugar

110g 'liquefied' egg
whites (see page 11)

1g approx. lemon yellow
food colouring

2g approx. pistachio green
food colouring

+

300g caster sugar

75g mineral water

110g 'liquefied' egg
whites (see page 11)

When making the basil juice, make sure you blend the leaves as finely as possible and stick rigidly to the temperatures indicated in the recipe, otherwise you could spoil the flavour.

The day before, prepare the basil juice and the lime and basil cream. Rinse the basil leaves then immerse them in boiling water for 5 minutes. Drain them and put them straight into ice-cold water.

Bring the sugar and water to the boil. Take it off the heat. When it reaches 60°C, add the blanched basil leaves and drain. Use a hand blender to blend finely.

Soak the gelatine for 15 minutes in cold water to soften. In a bowl over a pan of barely simmering water, stir the eggs with the sugar, zest and the lime and basil juice until it reaches 83/84°C. Strain then add the drained gelatine. Use a hand blender to blend for 10 minutes. Add the ground almonds. Allow to cool down then pour the cream into a gratin dish. Press clingfilm over the surface of the cream. Store in the fridge until next day.

Next day, make the macaron shells. Sift together the icing sugar and ground almonds. Stir the food colouring into the first portion of liquefied egg whites. Pour them over the mixture of icing sugar and ground almonds but do not stir.

Bring the water and sugar to the boil at 118°C. When the syrup reaches 115°C, simultaneously start whisking the second portion of liquefied egg whites to soft peaks. When the sugar reaches 118°C, pour it over the egg whites. Whisk and allow to cool down to 50°C, then add the meringue to the almond-sugar mixture and fold in. Spoon the batter into a piping bag with a plain nozzle.

Pipe rounds of batter about 3.5 cm in diameter, spacing them 2 cm apart on baking trays lined with baking parchment.

Rap the trays on the work surface covered with a kitchen cloth. Leave to stand for 30 minutes until a skin forms on the shells.

Preheat the fan oven to 180°C. Put the trays in the oven and bake for 12 minutes quickly opening and shutting the oven door twice during cooking time. Out of the oven, slide the shells on to the work surface.

50g mineral water

10g large-leaf basil leaves

10g caster sugar

225g whole eggs

240g caster sugar

8g lime zest

160g lime juice

Basil juice prepared as
  described

5g gelatine leaves

60g ground almonds

Gently stir the lime and basil cream. Spoon it into a piping bag with a plain nozzle.

Pipe a generous mound of ganache on to half the shells. Top with the remaining shells.

Store the macarons for 24 hours in the fridge. Bring them back out 2 hours before serving.

THE ASSOCIATION OF FLAVOURS FOR THIS MACARON STARTED OUT AS A MINESTRONE OF FRESH FRUIT AND A SORBET THAT BROUGHT TOGETHER THE COOL, INTENSE FLAVOURS OF FRESH LIME AND BASIL. IN 1997, I ADAPTED THEM TO MAKE A MACARON.

MILK CHOCOLATE AND EARL GREY TEA MACARON

Milk chocolate and white tip Earl Grey tea

Makes about 72 macarons (or about 144 shells)

PREPARATION TIME:

about 1 hour

COOKING TIME:

about 25 minutes

STANDING TIME:

30 minutes

REFRIGERATION:

24 hours

FOR THE MACARON SHELLS

300g ground almonds

300g icing sugar

110g 'liquefied' egg whites (see page 11)

3 vanilla pods

1 heaped teaspoon white tip Earl Grey leaf tea

12g cacao pâte

3g approx. red food colouring

+

300g caster sugar

75g mineral water

110g 'liquefied' egg whites (see page 11)

FOR THE EARL GREY TEA GANACHE

385g liquid crème fraîche or whipping cream (35% fat)

25g white tip Earl Grey tea

400g Valrhona Jivara couverture or milk chocolate, 40% cocoa solids

70g butter

TO FINISH

White tip Earl Grey tea

THE SOOTHING FRAGRANCE OF A STEAMING CUP OF EARL GREY TEA ADAPTED TO A MACARON! THE SMOOTH, CREAMY CONSISTENCY OF MILK CHOCOLATE ADDS THE FINEST HARMONY AND DELICATE FLAVOURS TO THE TASTE OF TEA AND BERGAMOT. A PERFECT BLEND OF FLAVOURS.

Sift together the icing sugar and ground almonds. Finely chop the Earl Grey tea leaves. Split the vanilla pods in half and scrape out the seeds with the blade of a knife then add them to the mixture of icing sugar and ground almonds with the chopped tea.

Pour the first portion of liquefied egg whites over the icing sugar-almond mixture but do not stir. Bring the water and sugar to boil at 118°C. When the syrup reaches 115°C, simultaneously start whisking the second portion of liquefied egg whites to soft peaks. When the sugar reaches 118°C, pour it over the egg whites. Whisk and allow to cool down to 50°C, then fold the meringue into the almond-sugar mixture. Spoon the batter into a piping bag fitted with a plain nozzle.

Pipe rounds of batter about 3.5 cm in diameter, spacing them 2 cm apart on baking trays lined with baking parchment. Rap the trays on the work surface covered with a kitchen cloth. Sprinkle the shells lightly with Earl Grey tea leaves. Leave the shells to stand for at least 30 minutes until they form a skin.

Preheat the fan oven to 180°C then put the trays in the oven. Bake for 12 minutes quickly opening and shutting the oven door twice during cooking time. Out of the oven, slide the shells on to the work surface.

Preheat the fan oven to 180°C then put the trays into the oven. Bake for 12 minutes quickly opening and shutting the oven door twice during cooking time. Out of the oven, slide the shells on to the work surface.

For the tea ganache. Bring the cream to the boil. Off the heat, add the tea and cover with a lid. Allow to infuse for 3 minutes then strain the cream. Partially melt the chocolate in a bowl over a pan of barely simmering water. Pour the cream into the chocolate a third at a time. When the mixture reaches 60°C, add the butter and whisk to obtain a smooth ganache.

Pour the ganache into a gratin dish. Press clingfilm over the surface of the ganache. Leave to stand at room temperature until it thickens.

Spoon the ganache into a piping bag with a plain nozzle. Pipe a generous mound of ganache on to half the shells and top with the remaining shells.

Store the macarons in the fridge for 24 hours then bring them back out 2 hours before serving.

AZUR MACARON
Chocolate and yuzu

Makes about 72 macarons
(or about 144 shells)

PREPARATION TIME:

about 1 hour

COOKING TIME:

about 25 minutes

STANDING TIME:

30 minutes

REFRIGERATION:

2 hours + 24 hours

FOR THE MACARON SHELLS

300g ground almonds

300g icing sugar

115g 'liquefied' egg whites
(see page 11)

120g cacao pâte (or dark
chocolate, 100% cocoa
solids)

+

330g caster sugar

75g mineral water

115g 'liquefied' egg whites
(see page 11)

3g approx. carmine red food
colouring

FOR THE CHOCOLATE AND
YUZU GANACHE

300g Valrhona Manjari
couverture, 64% cocoa
solids

300g liquid crème fraîche or
whipping cream (35%
fat)

65g yuzu juice (in Japanese
shops) or lime juice

115g 'La Viette' butter
(sweet butter from
Charentes)

ORIGINALLY FROM CHINA, YUZU IS A JAPANESE CITRUS FRUIT WITH A POWERFUL FLAVOUR SOMEWHERE BETWEEN LEMON, MANDARIN ORANGE AND LIME. I DISCOVERED IT IN 1986 ON MY FIRST TRIP TO JAPAN. AT THE TIME, IT HAD NOT YET BEEN IMPORTED TO FRANCE BUT I MANAGED TO GET HOLD OF IT THROUGH MICHEL AND BÉNÉDICTINE BACHÈS, WHO ARE PASSIONATE TREE GROWERS.

Sift together the icing sugar with the ground almonds. Melt the cacao pâte at 50°C in a bowl over a saucepan of barely simmering water. Stir the food colouring into the first portion of fresh egg whites. Add them to the mixture of icing sugar and almonds but do not stir.

Bring the water and sugar to the boil at 118°C. When the syrup reaches 115°C, simultaneously start whisking the second portion of liquefied egg whites to soft peaks. When the sugar reaches 118°C, pour it over the egg whites. Whisk and allow the meringue to cool down to 50°C, then fold it into the almond-sugar mixture. Spoon the batter into a piping bag fitted with a plain nozzle. Pipe rounds of batter about 3.5 cm in diameter, spacing them 2 cm apart on baking trays lined with baking parchment. Rap the trays on the work surface covered with a kitchen cloth. Leave the shells to stand for at least 30 minutes until they form a skin.

Preheat the fan oven to 180°C then put the trays in the oven. Bake for 12 minutes quickly opening and shutting the oven door twice during cooking time. Out of the oven, slide the shells on to the work surface.

For the chocolate and yuzu ganache. Chop up the chocolate and melt it in a bowl over a pan of barely simmering water. Heat the yuzu juice to 45-50°C. Bring the cream to the boil. Pour the cream over the melted chocolate and stir, then add the yuzu juice. When the ganache reaches 60°C, add butter cut up into pieces. Stir to obtain a smooth ganache. Pour the ganache into a gratin dish. Press clingfilm over the surface of the ganache and set aside in the fridge for the ganache to thicken.

Spoon the ganache into a piping bag with a plain nozzle. Pipe a generous mound of ganache on to half the shells and top with the remaining shells.

Store the macarons in the fridge for 24 hours then bring them back out 2 hours before serving.

INCA MACARON

Avocado, banana and chocolate

Makes about 72 macarons
(or about 144 shells)

PREPARATION TIME:

the day before, 25 minutes;
next day, about 1 hour

COOKING TIME:

the day before, 2 hours;
next day about 25
minutes

STANDING TIME:

30 minutes

REFRIGERATION:

2 hours + 24 hours

FOR THE SQUARES OF
BITTER CHOCOLATE
GANACHE

110g Valrhona Guanaja
couverture, 70% cocoa
solids

110g liquid crème fraîche
or whipping cream (35%
fat)

50g 'La Viette' butter
(sweet butter from
Charentes)

FOR THE MACARON SHELLS

300g ground almonds

300g icing sugar

110g 'liquefied' egg whites
(see page 11)

The day before, prepare the semi-dried bananas, if you have not managed to buy any. Preheat the oven to 80°C. Peel then halve the bananas lengthwise. Sprinkle them with lemon juice. Lay them on a baking tray and put them in the oven to partially dry out for 2 hours. They should be semi-dry. Set aside to cool, then store them in an air-tight container.

Still the day before, prepare the squares of bitter chocolate ganache. Chop up the chocolate and melt it in a bowl over a pan of barely simmering water. Bring the cream to the boil then pour it over the chocolate a third at a time. When the mixture has cooled down to 60°C, add the butter. Stir to obtain a smooth ganache. Pour it into a gratin dish lined with clingfilm to a depth of 4 mm. Set aside in the fridge for 1 hour then transfer the dish to the freezer. Turn out the ganache and cut it into 1.5 cm squares. Return the squares to the freezer.

Next day, make the macaron shells. Sift together the icing sugar and ground almonds. Stir the food colouring into the first portion of liquefied egg whites. Pour them over the icing sugar-almond mixture but do not stir. Bring the water and sugar to the boil at 118°C. When the syrup reaches 115°C, simultaneously start whisking the second portion of liquefied egg whites to soft peaks. When the sugar reaches 118°C, pour it over the egg whites. Whisk and leave the meringue to cool down to 50°C, then fold it into the almond-sugar mixture. Spoon the batter into a piping bag fitted with a plain nozzle.

Pipe rounds of batter about 3.5 cm in diameter, spacing them 2 cm apart on baking trays lined with baking parchment. Rap the trays on the work surface covered with a kitchen cloth. Leave the shells to stand for at least 30 minutes until they form a skin.

I'VE ALWAYS LIKED GUACAMOLE, SO I DECIDED TO TRANSPOSE THE DELICIOUSLY CREAMY TEXTURE AND SLIGHTLY NUTTY FLAVOUR OF AVOCADO TO A DESSERT, ADDING THE PIQUANCY OF LEMON JUICE. I CHOSE TO MATCH IT WITH THE WONDERFUL BITTERNESS OF BITTER CHOCOLATE AND THE AROMA OF BANANA.

+

300g caster sugar

75g mineral water

110g 'liquefied' egg
whites (see page 11)

10g approx. lemon yellow
food colouring

FOR THE BANANA AND
AVOCADO COMPOTE

120g very ripe avocados

25g lemon juice

100g banana purée

30g orange juice

Zest of a quarter lime

3 drops of Tabasco sauce

Ground white pepper

FOR THE BANANA AND
AVOCADO GANACHE

60g semi-dried bananas
or 4 ripe bananas + 20g
lemon juice

265g Valrhona Ivoire
couverture or white
chocolate

215g banana and
avocado compote

90g liquid crème fraîche
or whipping cream
(35% fat)

TO FINISH

Gold leaf

or

Edible gold glitter (see
page 205)

The avocados need to be very ripe and you should buy them several days in advance and leave them to stand at room temperature wrapped in newspaper.

Whatever you do, don't buy the dried bananas that are sold in shops. They are too compact and chewy.

Preheat the fan oven to 180°C then put the trays in the oven. Bake for 12 minutes quickly opening and shutting the oven door twice during cooking time. Out of the oven, slide the shells on to the work surface. Lay a few gold leaves on the shells if you have not already sprinkled them with gold glitter.

For the banana and avocado compote. Cut up the semi-dried banana into small 60g cubes. Halve the avocados and scoop out the flesh. Weigh out 135g avocado and immediately sprinkle it with lemon juice. In the mixer, blend it with the banana purée, orange juice and a quarter of the lime zest to obtain a fine purée. Season with Tabasco sauce and 2 grinds of white pepper.

Chop up the chocolate and melt it in a bowl over a pan of barely simmering water. Bring the cream to the boil. Pour it over the melted chocolate then add the banana and avocado compote. When the ganache is smooth, add and stir in the cubes of semi-dried banana. Tip the mixture into a gratin dish. Press clingfilm over the surface of the ganache and set aside in the fridge for the ganache to thicken.

Spoon the ganache into a piping bag with a plain nozzle. Pipe a generous mound of ganache on to half the shells. Gently press a square of frozen ganache into the centre then top with the remaining shells.

Store the macarons in the fridge for 24 hours then bring them back out 2 hours before serving.

TOUT PARIS MACARON

Dark and milk chocolate, caramel and Rice Krispies

Makes about 72 macarons
(or about 144 shells)

PREPARATION TIME:

about 1 hour

COOKING TIME:

about 35 minutes

STANDING TIME:

30 minutes

REFRIGERATION:

2 hours + 24 hours

FOR THE MACARON
SHELLS

300g ground almonds

300g icing sugar

120g cacao pâte or 100%
chocolate

110g 'liquefied' egg whites
(see page 11)

+

330g caster sugar

75g mineral water

110g 'liquefied' egg whites
(see page 11)

6g approx. carmine red
food colouring

FOR THE CRUNCHY
CARAMELISED RICE
KRISPIES SQUARES

120g caster sugar

30g water

80g Kellogg's Rice Krispies

100g Gianduja (see page
203)

150g Valrhona Caraïbe
chocolate, 66% cocoa
solids

In the cake of the same name I use pain d'épices (French gingerbread). If you can get hold of them, you can use 2 or 3g gingerbread spices in the macaron batter.

Start by making the caramelised Rice Krispie squares. Spread out the Rice Krispies in a frying pan and heat them to 60°C for a few minutes. Heat the sugar and water. When the syrup reaches 118°C, take it off the heat and add the hot Rice Krispies. Stir until the sugar crystallizes and whitens around the cereal. Return the pan to the heat. Stir over a medium heat until the Krispies caramelize and turn a deep amber colour. Spread the caramelised Rice Krispies on a lightly oiled baking tray. Allow to cool completely.

Chop up the chocolate and Gianduja and melt it in a bowl over a pan of barely simmering water. Take it off the heat, then add the cold caramelised Rice Krispies. Pour into a gratin dish lined with clingfilm to a depth of 4 mm. Smooth the surface with a spatula then set aside in the fridge to cool for 1 hour before transferring the dish to the freezer for 2 hours. Turn out the frozen mixture and cut into 1.5 cm squares. Return them to the freezer.

For the macaron shells. Sift together the icing sugar and ground almonds. Chop up the cacao pâte and melt it at 50°C in a bowl over a pan of barely simmering water. Stir the food colouring into the first portion of liquefied egg whites. Add this to the icing sugar-almond mixture but do not stir.

Bring the water and sugar to boil at 118°C. When the syrup reaches 115°C, simultaneously start whisking the second portion of liquefied egg whites to soft peaks. When the sugar reaches 118°C, pour it over the egg whites. Whisk and allow the meringue to cool down to 50°C then add it to the almond-sugar mixture, stir then fold in the melted cacao. Spoon the batter into a piping bag fitted with a plain nozzle.

Pipe rounds of batter about 3.5 cm in diameter, spacing them 2 cm apart on baking trays lined with baking parchment. Rap the trays on the work surface covered with a kitchen cloth. Sprinkle half the shells with 3 or 4 Rice Krispies and set aside for at least 30 minutes until they form a skin.

Preheat the fan oven to 180°C then slide the trays into

240g liquid crème fraîche
    or whipping cream
    (35% fat)

105g caster sugar

20g lightly salted 'La
    Viette' butter (sweet
    butter from Charentes)

260g Valrhona Caraibe
    couverture, 66% cocoa
    content

105g Valrhona Jivara
    couverture or milk
    chocolate, 40% cocoa
    solids

TO FINISH

Rice Krispies

the oven. Bake for 12 minutes quickly opening and shutting the oven door twice during cooking time. Out of the oven, slide the shells on to the work surface.

For the chocolate and caramel ganache. Bring the cream to the boil. Remove from the heat and melt the chopped chocolate in a bowl over a pan of barely simmering water. Tip half the sugar into a large saucepan and allow it to melt, then add the rest of the sugar. Heat until the sugar caramelises and turns a deep amber colour.

Take the pan off the heat and add the lightly salted butter, standing well back as the butter will bubble and spit. Stir with a spatula then pour in the hot cream a little at a time, stirring constantly. Bring to the boil to dissolve the particles of caramel. Pour the hot liquid over the melted chocolate a third at a time. Transfer the ganache into a gratin dish. Press clingfilm over the surface of the ganache and set aside in the fridge for the ganache to thicken. Spoon the ganache into a piping bag with a plain nozzle.

Pipe a generous mound of ganache on to half the shells. Gently press a frozen crunchy caramelised Rice Krispies square into the centre and top with the remaining shells.

Store the macarons in the fridge for 24 hours then bring them back out 2 hours before serving.

THE CHARM OF THIS MACARON IS IN THE CONTRASTING TEXTURES: THE CRISP AND CRUNCHY CARAMELISED RICE KRISPIES; THE SOFT, SILKY DARK AND MILK CHOCOLATE AND FINALLY THE CREAMY CARAMEL.

MILÉNA MACARON
Mint and raspberry

Makes about 72 macarons (or about 144 shells)

PREPARATION TIME:

the day before, 10 minutes; the next day, about 1 hour

COOKING TIME:

25 minutes

STANDING TIME:

30 minutes

REFRIGERATION:

2 hours + 24 hours

FOR THE MACARON SHELLS

300g ground almonds

300g icing sugar

110g 'liquefied' egg whites (see page 11)

10g approx. mint green food colouring

½ g egg yellow food colouring +

300g caster sugar

75g mineral water

110g 'liquefied' egg whites (see page 11)

FRESH MINT GANACHE

300g liquid crème fraîche or whipping cream (35% fat)

300g Valrhona Ivoire couverture or white chocolate

15g Get 27 peppermint liqueur

12g fresh mint leaves

120g ground almonds

FOR THE FILLING

About 40 fresh raspberries

TO FINISH

Chopped almonds

A few drops of carmine red food colouring

AN OSMOSIS OF INTENSE FRESH FLAVOURS: FRESH MINT AND THE SHARP ACIDITY OF FRESH RASPBERRY.

The day before, prepare the coloured chopped almonds. Wearing disposable gloves, mix the food colouring with the almonds. Spread them out in a single layer on a baking tray. Allow to dry at room temperature. Sift together the icing sugar and ground almonds. Stir the food colouring into the first portion of liquefied egg whites. Add them to the mixture of icing sugar and ground almonds but do not stir. Bring the water and sugar to boil at 118°C. When the syrup reaches 115°C, simultaneously start whisking the second portion of liquefied egg whites to soft peaks. When the sugar reaches 118°C, pour it over the egg whites. Whisk and allow the meringue to cool down to 50°C, then fold it into the almond-icing sugar mixture. Spoon the batter into a piping bag fitted with a plain nozzle.

Pipe rounds of batter about 3.5 cm in diameter, spacing them 2 cm apart on baking trays lined with baking parchment. Rap the trays on the work surface covered with a kitchen cloth. Sprinkle the shells with the coloured chopped almonds and set aside for 30 minutes until they form a skin.

Preheat the fan oven to 180°C then put the trays in the oven. Bake for 12 minutes quickly opening and shutting the oven door twice during cooking time. Out of the oven, slide the shells on to the work surface.

For the mint ganache. Remove the mint leaves from the stalks, then rinse and dry them. Chop them finely. Bring the cream to the boil then take it off the heat. Add the chopped mint and infuse for no more than 10 minutes without a lid. Strain the cream and retain the chopped mint. Blend it finely in the bowl of a food processor. Chop up the chocolate then melt it in a bowl over a pan of barely simmering water. Pour the hot cream infusion over the chocolate a third at a time. Add the chopped mint, the Get 27 peppermint liqueur and the ground almonds. Stir then spoon the ganache into a piping bag with a plain nozzle. Pipe a mound of the ganache on to half the shells. Gently press half a raspberry into the centre. Pipe another dot of ganache on top then cover with the remaining shells.

Store the macarons in the fridge for 24 hours then bring them back out 2 hours before serving (the same day or next day).

Make sure you don't cover the pan of infusing mint leaves, and don't allow them to infuse for more than 10 minutes to preserve the keen mint flavour in the ganache. Mint tastes of dried grass when it has been infused for too long. With its fresh raspberry in the centre, this macaron should be consumed within 48 hours of baking.

CHUAO MACARON

Chuao chocolate and blackcurrant

Makes about 72 macarons
(or about 144 shells)

PREPARATION TIME:

the day before, 10 minutes;
the next day, about 1
hour

COOKING TIME:

30 minutes

STANDING TIME:

30 minutes

REFRIGERATION:

2 hours + 24 hours

FOR THE MACARON SHELLS

300g ground almonds

300g icing sugar

120g cacao pâte (or dark
chocolate, 100% cocoa
solids)

115g 'liquefied' egg whites
(see page 11)

2g approx. carmine red
food colouring

+

300g caster sugar

75g mineral water

115g 'liquefied' egg whites
(see page 11)

The day before, defrost the 200g blackcurrants in a colander, if you are using frozen fruit, then dry them by spreading them out on paper towels. Blend with a hand blender then strain the purée you obtain. Store it in the fridge until next day.

Still the day before, bring 200g water to the boil with the sugar. Add the 200g fresh or frozen blackcurrants to the boiling syrup. Bring them back to the boil then take them off the heat and allow to macerate till next day.

The next day, make the macarons. Sift together the icing sugar and ground almonds. Chop up the cacao pâte and melt it at 50°C in a bowl over a pan of barely simmering water. Stir the food colouring into the first portion of liquefied egg whites. Add to the icing sugar-almond mixture but do not stir.

Bring the water and sugar to boil at 118°C. When the syrup reaches 115°C, simultaneously start whisking the second portion of liquefied egg whites to soft peaks. When the sugar reaches 118°C, pour it over the egg whites. Whisk and allow the meringue to cool to 50°C, then add it to the almond-icing sugar mixture, stir, then fold in the melted cacao pâte.

Crumble the crystallised violets. Spoon the macaron batter into a piping bag fitted with a plain nozzle.

I ROSE TO THIS CHALLENGE WHEN I HEARD ONE OF MY FELLOW CHOCOLATIERS SAY THAT BLACKCURRANT WAS THE ONLY FRUIT HE HAD NEVER MANAGED TO PAIR WITH CHOCOLATE. AND IT'S TRUE, APART FROM LIQUEUR CHOCOLATES, I HAD NEVER COME ACROSS THE COMBINATION. WHEN I FIRST TASTED THE FAINTLY MINTY FLAVOUR OF CHUAO CHOCOLATE, I WORKED ON THE ASSOCIATION TO HARNESS THE SHARP BITTERNESS AND ACIDITY OF THE TWO INGREDIENTS. I FIRST CAME UP WITH A CHUAO CAKE AND THEN THE CHUAO MACARON. THE SUCCESS OF MY ENDEAVOUR IS THANKS TO THE UNIQUE QUALITY OF THIS CHOCOLATE FROM VENEZUELA. IT CONTAINS CRIOLLO BEANS WHICH ARE SAID TO BE THE FINEST BEANS IN THE WORLD, TOGETHER WITH PORCELANA BEANS FROM LAKE MARACIBO.

30g cassis liqueur

200g fresh or frozen
blackcurrants

55g mineral water

10g lemon juice

20g caster sugar

210g Amedei Chuao pure
couverture (available
from delicatessens)

185g 'La Viette' butter
(sweet butter from
Charentes)

FOR THE FILLING

200g fresh or frozen
blackcurrants

200g water

100g caster sugar

TO FINISH

Dried cornflower petals or
crystallised violets

Pipe rounds of batter about 3.5 cm in diameter, spacing them 2 cm apart on baking sheets lined with baking parchment. Rap the trays on the work surface covered with a kitchen cloth. Sprinkle the shells with dried cornflowers or tiny pieces of crystallised violets and set aside for at least 30 minutes until they form a skin.

Preheat the fan oven to 180°C then put the trays in the oven. Bake for 12 minutes quickly opening and shutting the oven door twice during cooking time. Out of the oven, slide the shells on to the work surface.

For the chocolate ganache. Chop up the chocolate and melt it in a bowl over a pan of barely simmering water. Heat the blackcurrant purée with the liqueur, the water, lemon juice and the sugar. Turn out the heat under the pan just before it boils. Pour it over the chocolate a third at a time. When the mixture has cooled down to 60°C, add the butter. Stir to obtain a smooth ganache. Pour it into a gratin dish. Set aside in the fridge for 1 hour until it thickens.

Spoon the ganache into a piping bag fitted with a plain nozzle. Place the blackcurrants on paper towels to dry them 1 hour before filling the macarons. Pipe a generous mound of ganache on to half the shells. Lightly press 2 or 3 blackcurrants into the centre. Top with the remaining shells.

Store in the fridge for 24 hours and bring back out 2 hours before serving.

STRAWBERRY AND VANILLA MACARON

Makes about 72 macarons (or about 144 shells)

PREPARATION TIME:

the day before, 10 minutes; the next day, about 1 hour

COOKING TIME:

25 minutes

STANDING TIME:

30 minutes

REFRIGERATION:

2 hours + 24 hours

FOR THE STRAWBERRY COMPOTE

350g strawberries

20g lemon juice

25g caster sugar

3g gelatine leaves

FOR THE MACARON SHELLS

300g ground almonds

300g icing sugar

110g 'liquefied' egg whites (see page 11)

3 vanilla pods

+

300g caster sugar

75g mineral water

110g 'liquefied' egg whites (see page 11)

My favourite strawberries are Mara des Bois or Gariguette. They are often the ones with the greatest flavour.

The day before, prepare the coloured sugar to decorate the macarons. Preheat the oven to 60°C. Stir a few drops of colouring into the sugar, then, wearing disposable gloves, rub the mixture between the palms of your hands. Spread out the coloured sugar on a baking tray and place it in the oven to dry for 30 minutes.

For the strawberry compote. Soak the gelatine in cold water to soften. Rinse, dry and hull the strawberries. Process the strawberries using a hand blender (using the 'pulse' action) then press the mixture through a sieve to remove the seeds and add the lemon juice and sugar.

Warm a quarter of the strawberry purée to 35/40°C. Add the drained and dried gelatine leaves. Add the rest of the strawberry purée and stir briskly. Line a gratin dish with clingfilm and pour in the purée to a depth of 4 mm. Set aside in the fridge to cool for an hour then transfer the dish to the freezer for 2 hours. Turn out the compote and cut into 1.5 cm squares. Return the squares to the freezer.

For the macaron shells. Sift together the icing sugar and ground almonds. Split the vanilla pods, scrape out the seeds with the blade of a knife and add them to the mixture of icing sugar and ground almonds, then pour in the first portion of liquefied egg whites but do not stir.

Bring the water and sugar to boil at 118°C. When the syrup reaches 115°C, simultaneously start whisking the second portion of liquefied egg whites to soft peaks. When the sugar reaches 118°C, pour it over the egg whites. Whisk and allow the meringue to cool to 50°C, then add it to the almond-icing sugar mixture. Spoon the batter into a piping bag fitted with a plain nozzle.

Pipe rounds of batter about 3.5 cm in diameter, spacing them 2 cm apart on baking trays lined with baking parchment. Rap the trays on the work surface covered with a kitchen cloth. Sprinkle half the shells with granulated sugar using your fingertips and set aside for at least 30 minutes until they form a skin.

335g liquid crème fraîche
  or whipping cream
  (35% fat)

2 Mexican vanilla pods

2 Madagascan vanilla pods

2 Tahitian vanilla pods

375g Valrhona Ivoire
  couverture or white
  chocolate

TO FINISH

Granulated sugar

A few drops strawberry red
  food colouring

Preheat the fan oven to 180°C then put the trays in the oven. Bake for 12 minutes quickly opening and shutting the oven door twice during cooking time. Out of the oven, slide the shells on to the work surface.

For the vanilla ganache. Split the vanilla pods in two and scrape out the seeds with the blade of a knife. Stir them into the liquid crème fraîche or whipping cream (35% fat) with the scraped out vanilla pods. Bring the cream to the boil. Off the heat, cover and leave to infuse for 30 minutes.

Chop up the chocolate and melt it in a bowl over a pan of barely simmering water. Remove the vanilla pods from the cream and dry them carefully. Pour the cream a third at a time over the melted chocolate. Transfer to a gratin dish and set aside to cool.

Spoon the ganache into a piping bag with a plain nozzle. Pipe a generous mound of ganache on to half the shells then gently press a square of strawberry jelly into the centre. Top with the remaining shells.

Store the macarons for 24 hours in the fridge and bring back out 2 hours before serving.

AN EXCLUSIVE MACARON THAT WAS ONLY AVAILABLE IN 2007 TO CLIENTS AT THE PIERRE HERMÉ BOUTIQUE PARIS IN THE DEPARTMENT STORE ISETAN IN SHINJUKU, TOKYO. THE JAPANESE LOVE THE TANGY FLAVOUR OF JUICY STRAWBERRIES, WHICH ARE THEIR FAVOURITE FRUIT. FOR THIS MACARON, I MATCHED THEM WITH THE SUAVE, DELICATE ACCENTS OF VANILLA.

CAFFÉ-CAFFÉ MACARON
Coffee and candied orange

Makes about 72 macarons
 (or about 144 shells)

PREPARATION TIME:

the day before, 15 minutes;
 the next day, about 1 hour

COOKING TIME:

about 1 hour 50 minutes

STANDING TIME:

30 minutes

REFRIGERATION:

2 hours + 24 hours

FOR THE CANDIED ORANGES

6 untreated seedless oranges

1 litre water

500g caster sugar

1 star anise

10 Sarawak black
 peppercorns

1 vanilla pod

4 tablespoons lemon juice

FOR THE MACARON SHELLS

300g ground almonds

300g icing sugar

110g 'liquefied' egg whites
 (see page 11)

15g Trablit coffee extract

1.5g approx. egg yellow food
 colouring

+

300g caster sugar

75g mineral water

110g 'liquefied' egg whites
 (see page 11)

The day before, wash and dry the oranges. Slice the top and bottom off each one. Using a knife, cut thick segments from top to bottom and trim away the peel and a good centimetre of the flesh. Immerse the segments in a pan of boiling water. When the water boils, cook them for 2 minutes then drain. Refresh under cold water. Repeat this step twice more and drain the orange slices.

Crush the peppercorns. Put them in a pan with the water, sugar, lemon juice, star anise and halved vanilla pods with the seeds scraped out. Bring to the boil over a low heat. Add the orange segments. Three-quarters cover the pan with a lid and simmer very gently for 1 hour 30 minutes. Pour the mixture into a bowl and allow to cool. Cover with clingfilm and set aside in the fridge until next day.

The next day, drain the candied orange zests for 1 hour in a sieve resting over a bowl. Dice the zests into cubes with 3 mm sides.

For the macaron shells. Sift together the icing sugar and ground almonds. Stir the coffee extract and food colouring into the first portion of liquefied egg whites. Pour them over the mixture of icing sugar and ground almonds but do not stir.

Bring the water and sugar to the boil at 118°C. When the syrup reaches 115°C, simultaneously start whisking the second portion of liquefied egg whites to soft peaks. When the sugar reaches 118°C, pour it over the egg whites. Whisk and leave the meringue to cool down to 50°C, then fold it into the almond-icing sugar mixture. Spoon the batter into a piping bag fitted with a plain nozzle.

Pipe rounds of batter about 3.5 cm in diameter, spacing them 2 cm

IT ISN'T EASY TO FIND INGREDIENTS TO PAIR WITH THE POWERFUL TASTE OF COFFEE. HOWEVER, IN 1994, AS I SAT BY THE WATER'S EDGE SIPPING A CUP OF COFFEE FLAVOURED WITH LEMON ZEST, THE IDEA CAME TO ME TO MARRY COFFEE WITH A TANGY CITRUS FRUIT. I SETTLED ON ORANGE, FIRST IN A DESSERT, THEN IN A CAKE AND FINALLY IN THIS MACARON.

FOR THE COFFEE GANACHE

400g liquid crème fraîche or
   whipping cream (35% fat)

400g Valrhona Ivoire
   couverture or white
   chocolate

20g ground coffee
   (Colombian or Ethiopian
   Mocca)

TO FINISH

Very finely ground coffee

You can buy ready-prepared
candied orange but it will be
a lot sweeter and less
flavourful. Ideally in this
recipe you should use 3
saucepans of boiling water
because the zests should be
poached 3 times in boiling
water.

apart on baking trays lined with baking parchment. Rap the trays on the work surface covered with a kitchen cloth. Sprinkle the shells with a pinch of finely ground coffee and set aside for at least 30 minutes until they form a skin.

Preheat the fan oven to 180°C then put the trays in the oven. Bake for 12 minutes quickly opening and shutting the oven door twice during cooking time. Out of the oven, slide the shells on to the work surface.

For the coffee ganache. Bring the cream to the boil. Add the ground coffee. Cover with a lid and infuse it for a few minutes, then strain it through a fine-mesh sieve. Chop up the chocolate and melt it in a bowl over a pan of barely simmering water. Pour the hot infused cream over the chocolate a third at a time. Stir to obtain a smooth ganache. Transfer to a gratin plate. Press clingfilm over the surface of the ganache and set aside in the fridge for the ganache to thicken.

Spoon the ganache into a piping bag with a plain nozzle. Pipe a generous mound of ganache on to half the shells. Lightly press 3 or 4 pieces of candied orange into the ganache then top with the remaining shells.

Store the macarons in the fridge for 24 hours and bring them back out 2 hours before serving.

MEDÉLICE MACARON

Lemon and flaky hazelnut praline

Makes about 72 macarons (or about 144 shells)

PREPARATION TIME:

the day before, about 30 minutes; next day, about 1 hour

COOKING TIME:

the day before, about 25 minutes; next day, about 25 minutes

STANDING TIME:

30 minutes

REFRIGERATION:

2 hours + 24 hours

FOR THE FLAKY HAZELNUT PRALINE SQUARES

20g whole hazelnuts with their skins

20g 'La Viette' butter (sweet butter from Charentes)

45g Valrhona Jivara or milk chocolate, 40% cocoa solids

65g hazelnut praline

100g Piedmont hazelnut paste or Nutella

85g Gavotte biscuits

FOR THE MACARON SHELLS

300g ground almonds

To preserve the crunchiness of the Gavotte biscuits, don't crumble them too finely.

The day before, prepare the lemon cream. Rinse, dry and pare the zest from the lemons. Rub together the zests and sugar between your hands. In a bowl, stir together the lemon juice, lemon sugar and eggs. Place the bowl over a pan of barely simmering water. Whisk until the mixture reaches 83/84°C.

Allow to cool to 60°C then add the butter cut into pieces. Use a hand blender to blend for 10 minutes. Add the ground almonds and stir with the spatula. Pour the cream into a gratin dish. Press clingfilm over the surface of the cream. Set aside in the fridge until next day.

Still the day before, prepare the praline squares. Preheat the oven to 170°C. Spread out the hazelnuts on a baking tray and put them in the oven. Roast the nuts for about 15 minutes. Tip the hot nuts into a wide-mesh sieve or a colander and roll them about to remove the skins. Put the nuts in a plastic bag and use a rolling pin to crush them into medium-sized pieces.

Chop up the chocolate then melt it in a bowl over a pan of barely simmering water. Add the chopped nut praline, the praline paste and the butter cut into pieces. Stir to a smooth consistency then add the hazelnut pieces and the crumbled Gavotte biscuits. Pour the mixture into a gratin dish lined with clingfilm to a depth of 4 mm. Chill in the fridge for 1 hour then transfer the dish to the freezer for 2 hours. Turn out the praline from the gratin dish and cut it into 1.5 cm squares. Return the squares to the freezer.

Next day, make the macaron shells. Sift together the icing sugar and ground almonds. Stir the food colouring into the first portion of fresh egg whites. Add to the mixture of icing sugar and ground almonds but do not stir.

Bring the water and sugar to boil at 118°C. When the syrup reaches 115°C, simultaneously start whisking the second portion of liquefied egg whites to soft peaks. When the sugar reaches 118°C, pour it over the egg whites. Whisk and allow the meringue to cool down to 50°C, then fold it into the almond-icing sugar mixture. Spoon the batter into a piping bag with a plain nozzle.

300g icing sugar

110g 'liquefied' egg whites
(see page 11)

3g approx. lemon yellow
food colouring

1.5g approx. egg yellow
food colouring

+

300g caster sugar

75g mineral water

110g 'liquefied' egg whites
(see page 11)

225g whole fresh eggs

240g caster sugar

8g zest of Menton lemons
(or untreated organic
lemons)

160g fresh lemon juice

350g 'La Viette' butter

100g ground almonds

Gavotte biscuits

Pipe rounds of batter about 3.5 cm in diameter, spacing them 2 cm apart on baking trays lined with baking parchment. Rap the trays on the work surface covered with a kitchen cloth. Sprinkle the shells with crumbled Gavotte biscuits and set aside for about 30 minutes until they form a skin.

Preheat the fan oven to 180°C then put the trays in the oven. Bake for 12 minutes quickly opening and shutting the oven door twice during cooking time. Out of the oven, slide the shells on to the work surface. Stir the cream gently before spooning it into a piping bag with a plain nozzle.

Pipe a generous mound of ganache on to half the shells. Gently press a hazelnut praline square into the centre then top with the remaining shells.

Store the macarons in the fridge for 24 hours and bring back out 2 hours before serving.

BOTH CLASSIC AND ARRESTING, LEMON AND CRUNCHY HAZELNUT PRALINE TOGETHER MAKE A SUBTLE MARRIAGE. I FIRST USED THE ASSOCIATION IN A TART THEN IN A CAKE IN 1993. WHEN I THOUGHT ABOUT ADAPTING IT TO A MACARON IN 2002, I EMPHASISED THE AROMA RATHER THAN THE ACIDITY OF THE LEMON AND ADDED THE SWEET ROASTED FLAVOUR OF NUTELLA. THIS MACARON HAS NEVER BEEN SOLD IN PIERRE HERMÉ SHOPS IN PARIS: IT WILL BE ONE DAY...

ROSEHIP AND CHESTNUT MACARON

Makes about 72
  macarons (or about
  144 shells)

PREPARATION TIME:

about 1 hour 30
  minutes

COOKING TIME:

55 minutes

STANDING TIME:

30 minutes

REFRIGERATION:

2 hours + 24 hours

FOR THE WHITE
MACARON SHELLS

150g ground almonds

150g icing sugar

55g 'liquefied' egg
  whites (see page 11)

10g titanium oxide
  powder diluted in
  5g warm mineral
  water

+

150g caster sugar

38g mineral water

55g 'liquefied' egg
  whites (see page 11)

For the coloured sugar. Preheat the oven to 60°C. Stir a few drops of colouring into the sugar, then, wearing disposable gloves, rub the mixture between the palms of your hands. Spread out the coloured sugar on a baking tray and put it in the oven to dry for 30 minutes.

For the white shells. Sift together the icing sugar and ground almonds. Dilute the titanium oxide powder in the warm mineral water then stir it into the first portion of liquefied egg whites. Add them to the mixture of icing sugar and ground almonds but do not stir.

Bring the water and sugar to the boil at 118°C. When the syrup reaches 115°C, simultaneously start whisking the second portion of liquefied egg whites to soft peaks. When the sugar reaches 118°C, pour it over the egg whites. Whisk and allow the meringue to cool down to 50°C, then fold it into the almond-sugar mixture. Spoon the batter into a piping bag with a plain nozzle.

Pipe rounds of batter about 3.5 cm in diameter, spacing them 2 cm apart on baking trays lined with baking parchment. Rap the trays on the work surface covered with a kitchen cloth. Sprinkle with little pinches of coloured sugar or silver glitter. Leave the shells to stand for at least 30 minutes until they form a skin.

For the chestnut shells. Sift together the icing sugar and ground almonds. Chop up the cacao pâte and melt it at 50°C in a bowl over a pan of barely simmering water. Stir the chestnut purée and food colouring into the first portion of liquefied egg whites. Add them to the sugar-almond

A MEMORY IN A MACARON! MY FATHER GEORGES, A BAKER AND PASTRY CHEF IN COLMAR, USED TO MAKE A TRADITIONAL SPECIALITY OF ALSACE CALLED 'LA TORCHE AUX MARRONS' ('CHESTNUT TORCHES') THAT CONSISTED OF MERINGUE, CHANTILLY CREAM AND CHESTNUT CREAM. IN PARIS, THE SAME CAKE IS CALLED 'LE MONT BLANC'. MY PERSONAL TOUCH IS TO ADD ROSEHIP COMPOTE FOR A DELICATE NOTE OF FRESHNESS THAT ENLIVENS THE CHESTNUT FLAVOUR.

150g ground almonds

150g icing sugar

30g cacao pâte or dark
chocolate, 100%
cocoa solids

50g liquefied egg whites
(see page 11)

1.5g approx. carmine red
food colouring

+

150g caster sugar

38g mineral water

60g 'liquefied' egg
whites (see page 11)

FOR THE ROSEHIP

GANACHE

300g rosehip purée (see
page 204)

415g Valrhona Ivoire
couverture or white
chocolate

80g strawberries

TO FILL

A dozen chestnuts,
vacuum-packed or
bottled

TO FINISH

100g granulated sugar

A few drops carmine red
food colouring or

Edible bronze glitter (see
page 205) for the
chestnut macaron
shells

And edible silver glitter
(see page 205) for the
white shells

mixture but do not stir.

Bring the water and sugar to boil at 118°C. When the syrup reaches 115°C, simultaneously start whisking the second portion of liquefied egg whites to soft peaks. When the sugar reaches 118°C, pour it over the egg whites. Whisk and allow the meringue to cool to 50°C, then add it to the almond-sugar mixture, stir then fold in the melted cacao. Pour it into a piping bag fitted with a plain nozzle.

Pipe rounds of batter about 3.5 cm in diameter, spacing them 2 cm apart on baking trays lined with baking parchment. Rap the trays on the work surface covered with a kitchen cloth. Sprinkle with little pinches of coloured sugar or bronze glitter. Leave the shells to stand for at least 30 minutes until they form a skin.

Preheat the fan oven to 180°C then slide the trays into the oven. Bake for 12 minutes quickly opening and shutting the oven door twice during cooking time. Out of the oven, slide the shells on to the work surface.

For the rosehip ganache. Rinse, dry and hull the strawberries. Blend them with a hand blender then strain the purée you obtain.

Chop up the chocolate then melt it in a bowl over a pan of barely simmering water. Bring the rosehip purée together with the strawberry purée to the boil. Pour it over the chocolate a third at a time. Transfer the ganache to a gratin dish. Press clingfilm over the surface of the ganache and set aside in the fridge for the ganache to thicken.

Roughly chop the vacuum-cooked or bottled chestnuts. Spoon the ganache into a piping bag with a plain nozzle.

This works just as well if you make a single macaron batter. In autumn and winter, chestnut vacuum-cooked or bottled chestnuts are readily available in supermarkets or delicatessens.

Pipe a generous mound of ganache on to half the shells. Press three pieces of chestnut into the centre. Top with the remaining shells.

Store the macarons in the fridge for 24 hours then bring them back out 2 hours before serving.

FRIVOLITÉ MACARON
Salted-butter caramel and apple

Makes about 72 macarons
(or about 144 shells)

PREPARATION TIME:

the day before, 30
minutes; next day about
1 hour

COOKING TIME:

the day before, about 1
hour; next day, about 25
minutes

STANDING TIME:

30 minutes

REFRIGERATION:

24 hours

FOR THE SEMI-DRIED
APPLES

4 or 5 apples (Russet,
Cox's Orange or Granny
Smith)

30g lemon juice

20g caster sugar

FOR THE MACARON
SHELLS

300g ground almonds

300g icing sugar

110g 'liquefied' egg whites
(see page 11)

15g approx. egg yellow
food colouring

15g Trablit coffee extract

+

300g caster sugar

75g mineral water

110g 'liquefied' egg whites
(see page 11)

The day before, prepare the semi-dried apples. Peel and core the apples. Cut them into 8 mm cubes, sprinkling them immediately with lemon juice as you go along. Stir them into the sugar.

Preheat the oven to 90°C. Spread the cubes of apple out on a baking tray. Put them in the oven and dry them for about 1 hour according to the variety of apples you are using. The cubes should look slightly dry. Store them at room temperature until next day.

Next day, make the macaron shells. Sift together the icing sugar and ground almonds. Stir the food colouring into the first portion of fresh egg whites. Pour them into the mixture of icing sugar and ground almonds but do not stir.

Bring the water and sugar to boil at 118°C. When the syrup reaches 115°C, simultaneously start whisking the second portion of liquefied egg whites to soft peaks. When the sugar reaches 118°C, pour it over the egg whites. Whisk and allow the meringue to cool down to 50°C, then fold it into the almond-icing sugar mixture. Spoon the batter into a piping bag fitted with a plain nozzle.

Pipe rounds of batter about 3.5 cm in diameter, spacing them 2 cm apart on baking trays lined with baking parchment. Rap the trays on the work surface covered with a kitchen cloth. Sprinkle the shells with pinches of granulated sugar and set aside for at least 30 minutes until they form a skin.

Preheat the fan oven to 180°C then slide the trays into the oven. Bake for 12 minutes quickly opening and shutting the oven door twice during cooking time. Out of the oven, slide the shells on to the work surface.

For the salted-butter caramel cream. Bring the cream to the boil. Pour about 50g sugar into a large saucepan. Allow it to melt the sugar then add another 50g sugar and repeat this step 4 more times. Allow to caramelise until the caramel turns a very dark amber colour.

Take the pan off the heat. Add the 65g lightly salted butter, standing back as the mixture will bubble and spit. Stir with a spatula then pour in the cream a little at a time, stirring continually. Return the pan to a low heat. Heat the caramel until it reaches 108°C. Pour it into a gratin dish and

300g caster sugar

335g liquid crème fraîche
or whipping cream
(35% fat)

65g slightly softened,
lightly salted 'La Viette'
butter (sweet butter
from Charentes)

+ 290g softened 'La Viette'
butter

Granulated sugar

press clingfilm over the surface. Set aside in the fridge until it is cold.

In an electric mixer fitted with a whisk attachment, whisk the butter for 8 minutes to make it light and frothy. Briskly whisk in the cooled cream. Spoon the cream immediately into a piping bag with a plain nozzle.

Pipe a generous mound of the ganache on to half the shells. Gently press 5 or 6 cubes of semi-dried apples into the centre, then top with the remaining shells.

Store the macarons in the fridge for 24 hours and bring back out 2 hours before serving.

MY AIM WAS TO RECREATE A MACARON THAT TASTED LIKE A TRADITIONAL TARTE TATIN, ENCASING CUBES OF SEMI-DRIED APPLES IN A SMOOTH CREAM WITH THE INTENSE FLAVOUR OF SALTED-BUTTER CARAMEL.

MUTINÉ MACARON
Milk chocolate and coconut

THIS IS A WHIMSICAL DELICACY BASED ON THE BOUNTY BAR. TRANSPOSING THE TASTE OF A DELICIOUS MASS-PRODUCED CHOCO-LATE BAR TO A MACARON WAS SOMETHING OF A CHALLENGE! I ROAS-TED THE GRATED COCONUT THEN ADDED IT TO SMOOTH MILK CHOCO-LATE AND COCONUT MILK.

Makes about 72 macarons
(or about 144 shells)

PREPARATION TIME:

about 1 hour

COOKING TIME:

about 25 minutes

STANDING TIME:

30 minutes

REFRIGERATION:

2 hours + 24 hours

FOR THE MACARON SHELLS

300g ground almonds

300g icing sugar

150g grated coconut

90g 'liquefied' egg whites
(see page 11)

75g peanut oil

+

375g caster sugar

75g mineral water

180g 'liquefied' egg whites
(see page 11)

FOR THE MILK CHOCOLATE
AND COCONUT GANACHE

300g liquid crème fraîche or
whipping cream (35%
fat)

115g coconut milk

1½ vanilla pods

190g Valrhona Jivara
couverture or milk
chocolate, 40% cocoa
solids

150g grated coconut

TO FINISH

70g approx. ground coconut

Sift together the icing sugar and ground almonds. Pour the first portion of liquefied egg whites into the mixture of icing sugar and ground almonds together with the grated coconut and oil but do not stir.

Bring the water and sugar to boil at 118°C. When the syrup reaches 115°C, simultaneously start whisking the second portion of liquefied egg whites to soft peaks. When the sugar reaches 118°C, pour it over the egg whites. Whisk and allow the meringue to cool down to 50°C, then fold it into the almond-sugar mixture. Spoon the batter into a piping bag with a plain nozzle.

Pipe rounds of batter about 3.5 cm in diameter, spacing them 2 cm apart on baking trays lined with baking parchment. Rap the trays on the work surface covered with a kitchen cloth. Sprinkle the shells with coconut using your fingertips and set aside for at least 30 minutes until they form a skin.

Preheat the fan oven to 180°C then put the trays in the oven. Bake for 12 minutes quickly opening and shutting the oven door twice during cooking time. Out of the oven, slide the shells on to the work surface.

For the milk chocolate and coconut ganache. Preheat the oven to 160°C. Spread out the grated coconut on a baking tray and put it in the oven. Roast the coconut lightly for about 10 minutes. Bring to the boil the cream and the split vanilla pods with the seeds scraped out. Take the cream off the heat, cover and allow to infuse for 10 minutes. Chop up the chocolate and place it in a bowl. Strain the cream and return it to the heat, then pour it over the chocolate a third at a time. Add the coconut milk. Add the roasted coconut and stir. Pour the mixture into a gratin dish. Press clingfilm over the surface of the ganache and set aside in the fridge for the ganache to thicken.

Grated coconut soon turns rancid once the packet is open. To make sure it's fresh, I suggest storing it in the freezer and tasting it first before you use it.

Spoon the ganache into a piping bag fitted with a plain nozzle. Pipe a generous mound of ganache on to half the shells and top with the remaining shells.

Store the macarons in the fridge for 24 hours and bring back out 2 hours before serving.

TANGO MACARON

Raspberry, red pepper and Parmesan

Makes about 72
macarons (or about
144 shells)

PREPARATION TIME:

about 1 hour

COOKING TIME:

about 25 minutes

STANDING TIME:

30 minutes

REFRIGERATION:

2 hours + 24 hours

FOR THE MACARON
SHELLS

300g ground almonds

300g icing sugar

110g 'liquefied' egg
whites (see page 11)

30g approx. strawberry
red food colouring

Sift together the icing sugar and ground almonds.

Stir the food colouring into the first portion of fresh egg whites. Pour them over the mixture of nicing sugar and ground almonds but do not stir.

Bring the water and sugar to the boil at 118°C. When the syrup reaches 115°C, simultaneously start whisking the second portion of liquefied egg whites to soft peaks. When the sugar reaches 118°C, pour it over the egg whites. Whisk and allow the meringue to cool down to 50°C, then fold it into the almond-sugar mixture. Spoon the batter into a piping bag with a plain nozzle.

Pipe rounds of batter about 3.5 cm in diameter, spacing them 2 cm apart on baking trays lined with baking parchment. Rap the trays on the work surface covered with a kitchen cloth. Sprinkle the shells with a dusting of sifted ground almonds and set aside for at least 30 minutes until they form a skin.

IT WAS AT A SLOW FOOD FAIR IN THE EARLY YEARS OF THE MILLENNIUM, WHERE I WAS SAMPLING 'GRANDS CRUS' PARMESAN ACCOMPANIED BY FRUIT LIKE PEARS AND FIGS, THAT I CAME UP WITH THE IDEA OF USING IT IN A CAKE. RASPBERRY AND RED PEPPER SEEMED AN OBVIOUS PAIRING IN A SHORT-CRUST PASTRY TART OF RASPBERRY COMPOTE AND RED PEPPER WITH 'ROUGE' PARMESAN CREAM. I THEN HAD THE IDEA TO ADAPT THIS ASSOCIATION OF FLAVOURS TO A MACARON AND TO INCLUDE A DELICATE HINT OF PARMESAN IN A RASPBERRY AND RED PEPPER GANACHE.

SLOW FOOD IS AN ORGANISATION FOUNDED AND CHAIRED BY CARLO PETRINI. IT PROMOTES THE BENEFITS OF ETHICAL FOOD CONSUMPTION AND LOCALLY-SOURCED PRODUCE. IT RUNS COURSES ON THE SUBJECT OF TASTE, AMONG OTHER THINGS, FOR ADULTS AND CHILDREN, AND IT STRIVES TO SAFEGUARD AND PROMOTE CONSUMER CONSCIOUSNESS ABOUT CULINARY TRADITIONS TO COUNTERACT THE EXPANSION OF FAST FOOD.

+

300g caster sugar

75g mineral water

110g 'liquefied' egg
 whites (see page 11)

320g fresh raspberries

½ red pepper

300g Valrhona Ivoire
 couverture or white
 chocolate

50g ground almonds

TO FILL

About 40 fresh
 raspberries

About 80g 'Vacche
 Rosse' Parmesan (or
 top-quality
 Reggiano Parmesan)

TO FINISH

Ground almonds

A macaron to be eaten within 48 hours after the 24-hour standing time in the fridge.

'Vacche Rosse' Parmesan is a speciality cheese with a unique fruity flavour. It is made from the milk of a specific breed of cattle and is a 'Reggiano' that has been aged for 2 to 3 years. But it can be substituted by a high-quality Reggiano Parmesan.

Preheat the fan oven to 180°C then put the trays in the oven. Bake for 12 minutes quickly opening and shutting the oven door twice during cooking time. Out of the oven, slide the shells on to the work surface.

For the raspberry and red pepper ganache. Remove the seeds and white membranes from half a red pepper. Immerse it three times in boiling water then refresh in ice-cold water. Dry the red pepper. Remove the skin. Blend the pepper then sift it to a purée. Weigh out 30g pepper purée.

Blend the raspberry with a hand blender then strain the purée to remove the seeds. Weigh out 240g raspberry purée and stir it together with the pepper purée.

Chop up the chocolate then melt it in a bowl over a pan of barely simmering water. Heat the purée mixture to 40°C (no higher) then pour it over the chocolate a third at a time. Add the ground almonds.

Pour the ganache into a gratin dish. Press clingfilm over the surface of the ganache and set aside in the fridge for the ganache to thicken. Cut the Parmesan into little cubes with 5 mm sides

Pour the ganache into a piping bag fitted with a plain nozzle. Pipe mounds of ganache on to half the shells. Gently press half a raspberry and a cube of Parmesan into the centre. Finish with a dab of ganache then top them with the remaining shells.

Store the macarons in the fridge for 24 hours and bring back out 2 hours before serving. Consume the same day.

PLAISIR SUCRÉ MACARON
Milk chocolate and hazelnut

Makes about 72
  macarons (or about
  144 shells)

PREPARATION TIME:

about 1 hour

COOKING TIME:

about 40 minutes

STANDING TIME:

30 minutes

REFRIGERATION:

2 hours + 24 hours

FREEZING TIME:

2 hours

FOR THE MACARON
SHELLS

300g ground almonds

300g icing sugar

60g cacao pâte or dark
  chocolate, 100 %
  cocoa solids

110g 'liquefied' egg
  whites (see page 11)

10g coffee extract

20g approx. lemon
  yellow food colouring

+

300g caster sugar

75g mineral water

110g 'liquefied' egg
  whites (see page 11)

In this recipe, it is essential to use high quality milk chocolate. Too low a cocoa content will make the macaron too sweet.

Start by preparing the praline squares. Preheat the oven to 170°C. Spread out the hazelnuts on a baking tray. Put the tray in the oven and roast the nuts for about 15 minutes. Tip the hot nuts into a wide-mesh sieve or colander. Roll the nuts around to remove the skins then transfer the nuts to a plastic bag. Using a rolling pin, crush them into medium-sized pieces.

Chop up the chocolate and put it in a bowl over a pan of barely simmering water. Add in the chopped-nut praline, hazelnut paste and the butter cut into pieces. Stir to a smooth consistency then add the pieces of hazelnut and crumbled Gavotte biscuits.

Pour the praline into a gratin dish lined with clingfilm to a depth of 4 mm. Smooth the surface. Set aside in the fridge for 1 hour then transfer the dish to the freezer for 2 hours. Turn the slab out of the gratin dish and cut into 1.5 cm squares. Return the squares to the freezer.

For the macaron shells. Sift together the icing sugar and ground almonds. Melt the cacao pâte at 50°C in a bowl over a pan of barely simmering water. Stir the coffee extract and food colouring into the first portion of liquefied egg whites. Add to the mixture of icing sugar and ground almonds but do not stir.

Bring the water and sugar to the boil at 118°C. When the syrup reaches 115°C, simultaneously start whisking the second portion of liquefied egg whites to soft peaks. When the sugar reaches 118°C, pour it over the egg whites. Whisk and allow the meringue to cool down to 50°C, then add the meringue to the almond-sugar mixture, stir then fold in the melted cacao. Spoon the batter into a piping bag fitted with a plain nozzle.

Pipe rounds of batter about 3.5 cm in diameter, spacing them 2 cm apart on baking trays lined with baking parchment. Rap the trays on the work surface covered with a kitchen cloth. Crumble a few Gavotte biscuits between your fingers. Sprinkle the shells with biscuit crumbs and set aside for at least 30 minutes until they form a skin.

Preheat the fan oven to 180°C then put the trays in the oven. Bake for 12 minutes quickly opening and

20g whole hazelnuts with
their skins

20g 'La Viette' butter (sweet
butter from Charentes)

45g Valrhona Jivara
couverture or milk
chocolate, 40 % cocoa
solids

65g Nutella

100g Piedmont hazelnut
paste

85g Gavotte biscuits

FOR THE MILK CHOCOLATE
GANACHE

270g Valrhona Jivara
couverture or milk
chocolate, 40 % cocoa
solids

300g liquid crème fraîche or
whipping cream (35% fat)

TO FINISH

Gavotte biscuits

shutting the oven door twice during cooking time. Out of the oven, slide
the shells on to the work surface.

For the milk chocolate ganache. Chop up the chocolate and tip it into a
bowl. Bring the cream to the boil. Pour it over the chocolate a third at a
time. Transfer the ganache to a gratin dish. Press clingfilm over the surface
of the ganache and set aside in the fridge for the ganache to thicken. Spoon
the ganache into a piping bag fitted with a plain nozzle.

Pipe a mound of ganache on to half the shells. Lightly press a square of
the frozen hazelnut praline into the centre and finish with a dot of ganache.
Top with the remaining shells.

Store the macarons for 24 hours in the fridge. Bring them back out two
hours before serving.

WHEN I DISCOVERED VALRHONA JIVARA CHOCOLATE IN 1992, I WAS KEEN TO APPROPRIATE THE
CLASSIC COMBINATION OF MILK CHOCOLATE AND HAZELNUTS. AT THE TIME, THE CRAZE FOR BIT-
TER CHOCOLATE HAD REACHED ITS APOGEE AND MILK CHOCOLATE WAS OUT OF FAVOUR WITH
BOTH PROFESSIONALS AND GASTRONOMES. ANYONE WHO STILL LIKED IT DARED NOT OWN UP
OR HAD TO EAT IT ON THE SLY. I HAD ALSO DISCOVERED LINDOR, THOSE DELICIOUS LINDT CHO-
COLATES THAT CREATE AN INSTANT COOL SENSATION IN THE MOUTH. THEN I MET YANN PENNORS
AND CHARLES ZNATY (WITH WHOM I FOUNDED PIERRE HERMÉ, PARIS, A FEW YEARS LATER) AND
WE DESIGNED A CAKE THAT NO OTHER PASTRY CHEF WOULD EVER HAVE THOUGHT OF. IN 1993,
I PUT MY OWN INTERPRETATION ON THE RESULT AND REVISITED LINDOR CHOCOLATES. TO INTEN-
SIFY THE PLEASURE, I MINGLED THE SMOOTHNESS OF THE MILK CHOCOLATE FILLING WITH THE
CRUNCHINESS OF FLAKY HAZELNUT PRALINE. IT WAS THE MOST COMPLICATED CAKE I EVER
MADE IN TERMS OF TEXTURE AND SENSATION.

MADE-TO-ORDER MACARONS

'I DESIGNED SOME "HAUTE-COUTURE" MACARONS FOR AND WITH SPECIFIC CLIENTS.'

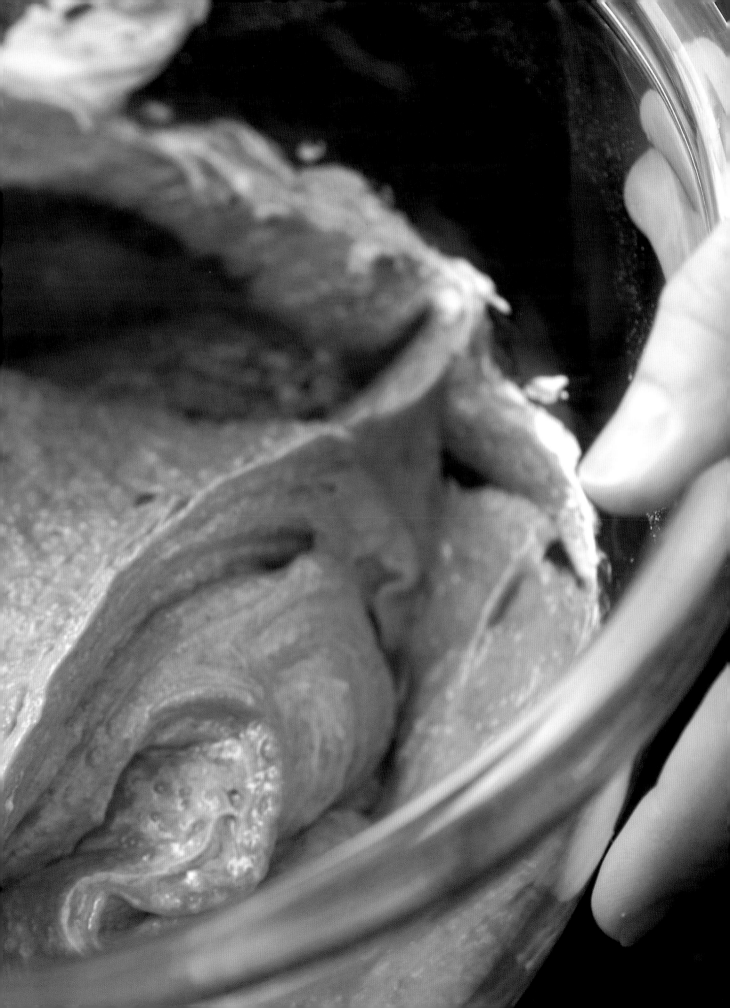

JASMINE MACARON

For Jean Patou perfumes

I CREATED THIS MACARON WITH THE HELP OF MY FRIEND AND 'HOUSE NOSE', JEAN-MICHEL DURIEZ, FOR THE LAUNCH OF THE PERFUME 'SIRA DES INDES' BY JEAN PATOU, IN 2005. I DISCOVERED ALL THE SUBTLETIES OF A FLAVOUR I HAD NOT YET USED AND I FOUND THE PURE, DELICATE FRAGRANCE OF JASMINE FLOWERS SO INTOXICATING THAT I DECIDED TO SELL IT IN PIERRE HERMÉ PARIS SHOPS.

Makes about 72 macarons (or about 144 shells)

PREPARATION TIME:

about 1 hour

COOKING TIME:

about 25 minutes

STANDING TIME:

30 minutes

REFRIGERATION:

2 hours + 24 hours

FOR THE MACARON SHELLS

300g ground almonds

300g icing sugar

110g 'liquefied' egg whites (see page 11)

15g titanium oxide powder

10g warm mineral water

+

300g caster sugar

75g mineral water

110g 'liquefied' egg whites (see page 11)

FOR THE JASMINE GANACHE

360g liquid crème fraîche or whipping cream (35% fat)

320g Valrhona Ivoire couverture or white chocolate

25g jasmine tea

TO FINISH

White granulated sugar

or

Dried jasmine petals

or

Edible silver glitter (see page 205)

Sift together the icing sugar and ground almonds.

Dilute the titanium oxide powder in a bowl of warm mineral water and stir it into the first portion of liquefied egg whites. Pour them over the mixture of icing sugar and ground almonds but do not stir.

Bring the water and sugar to boil at 118°C. When the syrup reaches 115°C, simultaneously start whisking the second portion of liquefied egg whites to soft peaks. When the sugar reaches 118°C, pour it over the egg whites. Whisk and allow the meringue to cool down to 50°C, then fold it into the almond-sugar mixture. Spoon the batter into a piping bag fitted with a plain nozzle.

Pipe rounds of batter about 3.5 cm in diameter, spacing them 2 cm apart on baking trays lined with baking parchment. Rap the trays on the work surface covered with a kitchen cloth. Sprinkle the shells with a dusting of granulated sugar, a few dried jasmine petals or edible silver glitter. Leave the shells to stand for at least 30 minutes until they form a skin.

Preheat the fan oven to 180°C then put the trays in the oven. Bake for 12 minutes quickly opening and shutting the oven door twice during cooking time. Out of the oven, slide the shells on to the work surface.

For the tea ganache. Heat the cream to 85°C. Off the heat, add the jasmine tea and cover with a lid. Allow to infuse for no more than 3 minutes. Strain the cream.

Chop up the chocolate and melt it in a bowl over a pan of barely simmering water. Pour the cream over the melted chocolate a third at a time. Transfer the mixture to a gratin dish. Press clingfilm over the surface of the ganache and set aside in the fridge for the ganache to thicken.

Spoon the ganache into a piping bag fitted with a plain nozzle. Pipe a generous mound of ganache on to half the shells and top with the remaining shells.

Store the macarons in the fridge for 24 hours then bring them back out 2 hours before serving.

We use Chinese jade pearl tea with jasmine. On the recommendation of my friend Jean-Michel Duriez, I add a few drops of Sambac jasmine essence, which he chose for me, to bring out the flavour of jasmine.

LEMON AND AVOCADO MACARON

Makes about 72 macarons (or about 144 shells)

PREPARATION TIME:

the day before, 15 minutes; next day, about 1 hour

COOKING TIME:

about 1 hour 50 minutes

STANDING TIME:

30 minutes

REFRIGERATION:

2 hours + 24 hours

FOR THE CUBES OF CANDIED LEMON

8 untreated lemons

1 litre water

500g caster sugar

1 star anise

10 Sarawak black peppercorns

1 vanilla pod

4 tablespoons lemon juice

FOR THE YELLOW MACARON SHELLS

150g ground almonds

150g icing sugar

55g 'liquefied' egg whites (see page 11)

5g drops egg yellow food colouring

5g lemon yellow food colouring

+

150g caster sugar

38g mineral water

55g 'liquefied' egg whites (see page 11)

The day before, wash and dry the lemons. Cut off both ends. Use a knife to cut thick segments from top to bottom of the fruit, trimming away the rind and a good centimetre of flesh.

Immerse the lemon segments in a pan of boiling water. Bring the water back to the boil, cook the lemon for 2 minutes then drain. Refresh the segments in cold water. Repeat this step twice more, then drain the lemon segments.

Grind the peppercorns. Put them in a saucepan with the water, sugar, lemon juice, the star anise and the split vanilla pod with the seeds scraped out. Bring to the boil on a low heat. Add the lemon slices, put a lid on the pan so that it is three-quarters covered and simmer very gently for 1 hour 30 minutes. Take off the heat and allow to cool. Cover with clingfilm and set aside in the fridge until next day.

Next day, drain the slices of candied lemon for 1 hour in a sieve over a bowl. Cut them into cubes with 3 mm sides.

For the macaron shells. Sift together the icing sugar and ground almonds. Stir the food colouring into the first portion of liquefied egg whites. Pour them over the mixture of icing sugar and ground almonds but do not stir.

Bring the water and sugar to boil at 118°C. When the syrup reaches 115°C, simultaneously start whisking the second portion of liquefied egg whites to soft peaks. When the sugar reaches 118°C, pour it over the egg whites. Whisk and allow the meringue to cool down to 50°C, then fold it into the almond-sugar mixture. Spoon the batter into a piping bag fitted with a plain nozzle.

Pipe rounds of batter about 3.5 cm in diameter, spacing them 2 cm apart on baking trays lined with baking parchment. Rap the trays on the work surface covered with a kitchen cloth. Leave the shells to stand for at least 30 minutes until they form a skin.

Preheat the fan oven to 180°C then put the trays in the oven. Bake for 12 minutes quickly opening and shutting the oven door twice during cooking time.

Keep any remaining cubes of candied lemon in an air-tight container in the fridge and consume within 2 weeks.

150g ground almonds

150g icing sugar

55g 'liquefied' egg
whites (see page 11)

1g approx. lemon yellow
food colouring

2g approx. pistachio
green food colouring

+

150g caster sugar

38g mineral water

55g 'liquefied' egg
whites (see page 11)

2 very ripe avocados (for
300g avocado purée)

50g lemon juice

100g liquid crème
fraîche or whipping
cream (35% fat)

The zest of half a lemon

500g Valrhona Ivoire
couverture or white
chocolate

Out of the oven, slide the shells on to the work surface.

For the lemon and avocado ganache. Halve the avocados, remove the stone and scrape out the flesh with a spoon. Blend and weigh out 300g. Sprinkle immediately with lemon juice. Heat the purée to 40/50°C in a small pan over a very low heat, stirring constantly.

Chop up the chocolate and melt it in a bowl over a pan of barely simmering water. Bring the cream to the boil. Add the zest of half a lemon. Pour the cream over the melted chocolate then add the avocado and lemon purée a little at a time. Transfer the mixture to a gratin dish. Press clingfilm over the surface of the ganache and set aside in the fridge for the ganache to thicken.

Spoon the ganache into a piping bag with a plain nozzle. Pipe a generous mound of ganache on to half the shells. Gently press 3 cubes of candied lemon into the ganache and top with the remaining shells.

Store the macarons in the fridge for 24 hours then bring them back out 2 hours before serving.

CARROT AND ORANGE MACARON

Makes about 72
    macarons (or about
    144 shells)

PREPARATION TIME:

about 1 hour 15
    minutes

COOKING TIME:

about 40 minutes

STANDING TIME:

30 minutes

REFRIGERATION:

2 hours + 24 hours

FOR THE MACARON
SHELLS

300g ground almonds

300g icing sugar

110g 'liquefied' egg
    whites (see page 11)

+

300g caster sugar

75g mineral water

110g 'liquefied' egg
    whites (see page 11)

7g approx. lemon
    yellow food
    colouring

1g approx. carmine red
    food colouring

1g strawberry red food
    colouring

Make sure the carrots are soft right through otherwise they will taste too much like vegetables. Taste them to check they are the right consistency before you take them off the heat.

Carrots need different cooking times according to the season. Early spring carrots need far less time than winter carrots.

The day before, make the filling. Peel the carrots then cut them into cubes with 5mm sides. Bring the water to the boil with the lemon and orange juice, the sugar, cinnamon and the orange zest. Add the carrots and cook until the carrots are soft right through. Take them off the heat and allow to marinate overnight.

Next day, sift together the icing sugar and ground almonds. Stir the food colouring into the first portion of liquefied egg whites. Pour them over the mixture of icing sugar and ground almonds but do not stir.

Bring the water and sugar to boil at 118°C. When the syrup reaches 115°C simultaneously start whisking the second portion of liquefied egg whites to soft peaks. When the sugar reaches 118°C, pour it over the egg whites. Whisk and allow the meringue to cool down to 50°C, then fold it into the almond-sugar mixture. Spoon the batter into a piping bag fitted with a plain nozzle.

Pipe rounds of batter about 3.5 cm in diameter, spacing them 2 cm apart on baking trays lined with baking parchment. Rap the trays on the work surface covered with a kitchen cloth. Leave the shells to stand for at least 30 minutes until they form a skin.

Preheat the fan oven to 180°C then put the trays in the oven. Bake for 12 minutes quickly opening and shutting the oven door twice during cooking time. Out of the oven, slide the shells on to the work surface.

Drain the cubes of carrot and pat dry with kitchen roll. Allow to drain before putting them in the fridge on kitchen roll.

For the orange and carrot ganache. Chop up the chocolate and melt it in a bowl over a pan of barely simmering water. Heat together the lemon juice, orange juice, the carrots and the finely zested orange to 45-50°C. Pour the juice over the melted chocolate a third at a time. Transfer the ganache to a gratin dish.

200g carrots

350g mineral water

120g lemon juice

25g orange juice

50g caster sugar

½ cinnamon stick

Zest of ¼ orange

FOR THE CARROT AND
ORANGE GANACHE

450g Valrhona Ivoire
    couverture or white
    chocolate

80g fresh orange juice
    with the pulp

Zest of half an orange

10g lemon juice

100g carrot juice (fresh
    or good quality
    bottled)

Press clingfilm over the surface of the ganache and set aside in the fridge for the ganache to thicken.

Spoon the ganache into a piping bag fitted with a plain nozzle. Pipe a generous mound of ganache on to half the shells. Gently press 4 cubes of carrot into the ganache and top with the remaining shells.

Store the macarons in the fridge for 24 hours then bring them back out 2 hours before serving.

A MADE-TO-ORDER CREATION FOR A BRAND OF FROZEN VEGETABLES WHEN IT LAUNCHED A NEW PRODUCT. I WAS INSPIRED BY A RECIPE FOR A CARROT AND ORANGE SALAD AMONG THIRTEEN MOROCCAN DISHES. I HAD ALREADY WORKED ON THIS MARRIAGE OF FLAVOURS FOR A RESTAURANT DESSERT IN 1998 – CARROT AND ORANGE SALAD WITH CINNAMON AND CARDAMOM ICE CREAM – AND LATER FOR A CAKE IN A GOBLET, FOR A HYBRID EXPERIENCE!

MACARON WITH KETCHUP
For Colette

THIS MACARON WAS MADE AT SARAH'S REQUEST TO CELEBRATE THE FIFTH BIRTHDAY OF THE OPENING OF THE BOUTIQUE COLETTE ON THE RUE SAINT HONORÉ IN PARIS. WORKING WITH A COMMERCIAL PRODUCT LIKE KETCHUP WITH ITS SPICY SWEET AND SOUR FLAVOUR WAS A CHALLENGE. THE ADDITION OF TINY PIECES OF CORNICHON BALANCES THE SWEET AND SAVOURY.

Makes about 72 macarons (or about 144 shells)

PREPARATION TIME:

about 1 hour

COOKING TIME:

about 25 minutes

STANDING TIME:

30 minutes

REFRIGERATION:

2 hours + 24 hours

FOR THE MACARON SHELLS

300g ground almonds

300g icing sugar

110g 'liquefied' egg whites (see page 11)

30g approx. strawberry red food colouring

+

300g caster sugar

75g mineral water

110g 'liquefied' egg whites (see page 11)

FOR THE KETCHUP FILLING

700g Heinz ketchup

12g gelatine leaves (2g each)

80g cornichons

8-10 drops Tabasco sauce

TO FINISH

Tomato powder (from specialist shops) or sun-dried tomatoes ground to a powder

Sift together the icing sugar and ground almonds. Stir the food colouring into the first portion of liquefied egg whites. Pour them over the mixture of icing sugar and ground almonds but do not stir.

Bring the water and sugar to boil at 118°C. When the syrup reaches 115°C, simultaneously start whisking the second portion of liquefied egg whites to soft peaks. When the sugar reaches 118°C, pour it over the egg whites. Whisk and allow the meringue to cool down to 50°C, then fold it into the almond-sugar mixture. Spoon the batter into a piping bag fitted with a plain nozzle.

Pipe rounds of batter about 3.5 cm in diameter, spacing them 2 cm apart on baking trays lined with baking parchment. Rap the trays on the work surface covered with a kitchen cloth. Sprinkle with a light dusting of tomato powder. Leave the shells to stand for at least 30 minutes until they form a skin.

Preheat the fan oven to 180°C then put the trays in the oven. Bake for 12 minutes quickly opening and shutting the oven door twice during cooking time. Out of the oven, slide the shells on to the work surface.

For the ketchup filling. Soak the gelatine in cold water for 15 minutes to soften. Drain and rinse the cornichons and pat them dry on kitchen roll. Dice the cornichons into tiny 1mm cubes.

Drain the gelatine and melt it in a bowl over a saucepan of barely simmering water or in the microwave. Add about a quarter of the ketchup and stir, then add the rest of the ketchup and the diced cornichons. Season with Tabasco sauce. Pour into a gratin dish and press clingfilm over the surface of the mixture. Set aside in the fridge for 2 hours.

Spoon the ketchup filling into a piping bag fitted with a plain nozzle.

Ketchups can vary enormously from one brand to another. I must admit, I definitely prefer Heinz ketchup.

Pipe a generous mound of filling on to half the macaron shells then top with the remaining shells.

Store the macarons in the fridge for 24 hours and bring back out 2 hours before serving.

PARIS-MATCH MACARON

Makes about 72 macarons
(or about 144 shells)

PREPARATION TIME:

about 1 hour

COOKING TIME:

about 35 minutes

STANDING TIME:

30 minutes

REFRIGERATION:

2 hours + 24 hours

FOR THE WHITE
MACARON SHELLS WITH A
RED DOT

150g ground almonds

150g icing sugar

55g 'liquefied' egg whites
(see page 11)

7.5g titanium oxide
powder + 5 g warm
mineral water

+

150g caster sugar

38g mineral water

55g 'liquefied' egg whites
(see page 11)

For the white macaron shells. Sift together the icing sugar and ground almonds. Dilute the titanium oxide powder in the warm mineral water then stir it into the first portion of liquefied egg whites. Pour them over the mixture of icing sugar and ground almonds but do not stir.

Bring the water and sugar to boil at 118°C. When the syrup reaches 115°C, simultaneously start whisking the second portion of liquefied egg whites to soft peaks. When the sugar reaches 118°C, pour it over the egg whites. Whisk and allow the meringue to cool down to 50°C, then fold it into the almond-sugar mixture. Spoon the batter into a piping bag fitted with a plain nozzle.

Pipe rounds of batter about 3.5 cm in diameter, spacing them 2 cm apart on baking trays lined with baking parchment. Rap the trays on the work surface covered with a kitchen cloth. Leave the shells to stand for at least 30 minutes until they form a skin.

For the red macaron shells. Sift together the icing sugar and ground almonds. Stir the food colouring into the first portion of liquefied egg whites. Pour them over the mixture of icing sugar and ground almonds but do not stir.

Bring the water and sugar to boil at 118°C. When the syrup reaches 115°C, simultaneously start whisking the second portion of liquefied egg whites to soft peaks. When the sugar reaches 118°C, pour it over the egg whites. Whisk and allow the meringue to cool down to 50°C, then fold it into the almond-sugar mixture. Spoon the batter into a piping bag with a plain nozzle.

Pipe rounds of batter about 3.5 cm in diameter, spacing them 2 cm

A MADE-TO-ORDER MACARON FOR PARIS-MATCH. IT CAME ABOUT IN THE FOLLOWING WAY: IN 2007, ANNE-MARIE CORRE, THE EXECUTIVE EDITOR, CONTACTED ME TO ASK ME FOR A MACA-RON THAT WOULD SYMBOLIZE HER MAGAZINE. WE BOTH CAME UP WITH THE SAME IDEA AT THE SAME TIME: THE RECIPE HAD TO INCLUDE ESPELETTE CHILLI PEPPER! DON'T ASK ME WHY: SOME INSTINCTS CAN'T BE ACCOUNTED FOR! I COMBINED THE TARTNESS OF RED PEPPER WITH THE JUICY, TANGY FLAVOUR OF RASPBERRY AND THE BITTERNESS OF DARK CHOCOLATE.

150g ground almonds

150g icing sugar

55g 'liquefied' egg whites
(see page 11)

10g strawberry red food
colouring

3g carmine red food
colouring

+

150g caster sugar

38g mineral water

55g 'liquefied' egg whites
(see page 11)

FOR THE CHOCOLATE
AND RASPBERRY GANACHE
WITH ESPELETTE CHILLI
PEPPER

Half a red pepper

330g fresh (or frozen)
raspberries

250g Valrhona Manjari
couverture, 64 % cocoa
solids

50g 'La Viette' butter
(sweet butter from
Charentes)

30g lightly salted 'La
Viette' butter

3g Espelette chilli pepper
powder

Espelette chilli peppers are named after a village in the Basque region of France. A native of South America, the plant was introduced to the Basque country in the 16th or 17th century. It was first used for its medicinal properties but was very soon added to flavour and preserve meat and ham. In 1650, Espelette pepper plants began to be farmed. The seeds were carefully selected and the Gorria variety was developed. These seeds are now known as 'piment d'Espelette', or Espelette chilli pepper. The chilli pepper carries the quality label 'Appellation d'origine contrôlée'.

apart on baking trays lined with baking parchment. Rap the trays on the work surface covered with a kitchen cloth.

Pipe a tiny red dot on the centre of the white shells using a plain No. 6 nozzle and a tiny white dot on the centre of the red shells. Rap the baking trays again on the work surface covered with a kitchen cloth. Leave the shells to stand for at least 30 minutes until they form a skin.

For the chocolate and raspberry ganache with Espelette chilli pepper. Remove the seeds and white membranes from half a pepper. Immerse it 3 times in boiling water then refresh in ice-cold water. Dry the red pepper. Remove the skin. Blend the pepper then force it through a sieve to obtain a smooth purée. Weigh out 35g of the pepper purée.

Blend the raspberries with a hand blender. Strain the purée. Stir 265g of the sifted raspberry purée with 35g pepper purée with Espelette chilli pepper.

Chop up the chocolate and melt it in a bowl over a pan of barely simmering water. Heat the purée mixture to 40°C but no higher, then pour it over the chocolate a third at a time. When the mixture reaches 60°C add the sweet and the lightly salted butter a little at a time. Whisk to obtain a smooth ganache.

Transfer the ganache to a gratin dish. Press clingfilm over the surface of the ganache and set aside in the fridge for the ganache to thicken.

Spoon the ganache into a piping bag fitted with a plain nozzle. Pipe a generous mound of ganache on to half the shells and top with the remaining shells.

Store the macarons in the fridge for 24 hours then bring them back out 2 hours before serving.

MANDARIN ORANGE MACARON WITH PINK PEPPERCORNS

Makes about 72 macarons
(or about 144 shells)

PREPARATION TIME:

the day before, 40
minutes; next day, about
1 hour

COOKING TIME:

the day before, about 10
minutes; next day, 12
minutes

STANDING TIME:

30 minutes

REFRIGERATION:

24 hours + 24 hours

FOR THE MANDARIN
ORANGE COMPOTE

6 or 7 mandarin oranges
for 270g juice

85g orange marmalade,
bottled

5g lump sugar

4g gelatine leaves

FOR THE MOUSSELINE
CREAM OF MANDARIN
ORANGE AND PINK
PEPPERCORNS

135g whole eggs

145g caster sugar

3 mandarin oranges

Zest of ¼ orange

5g cornflour

20g lemon juice

Zest of 3 mandarin
oranges

3 mandarins, for 85g juice

Make sure you buy fine-cut orange marmalade. The marmalade I use, made by Christine Ferber, a pastry chef in Niedermorshwihr in Alsace, is to die for!

Pink peppercorns are not related to peppers. They are the fruits that grow on a large South American tree with drooping branches that belongs to the anacardiaceae family, which includes mango and sumac. Its long clusters of berries make it look like a pepper tree. The fruit is harvested when ripe and then dried. The pink berries are pungent with a sweetish, mildly piquant flavour. In France, the berries are no longer referred to as 'pink peppercorns' since the French directorate for Fraud Control proved that it had a different origin from the pepper. A native of South America, it is today grown on Reunion Island, hence its French nickname 'Rose de La Réunion' (or Golden Rose of Reunion).

The day before, make the mandarin orange compote. Soak the gelatine for 15 minutes in cold water to soften. Rinse and dry the mandarin oranges then pare the zest using a Microplane grater. Squeeze the juice of the mandarins. Weigh out 270g juice then heat it to about 50°C with the orange marmalade.

Take off the heat and add the drained gelatine. Stir in the zests. Blend then pour into a gratin dish lined with clingfilm to a depth of 4 mm. Smooth the surface. Allow to cool in the fridge for 1 hour then transfer the dish to the freezer for 2 hours. Turn out the compote and cut it into 1.5 cm squares. Return the squares to the freezer.

Still the day before, prepare the mandarin orange cream with pink peppercorns. Rinse and dry the mandarin oranges. Pare the zest and squeeze the juice to obtain 85g juice. Pare the zest from the quarter orange. Stir the zests into the sugar and rub them together thoroughly.

In a bowl over a pan of barely simmering water, stir the eggs with the sugar and the mandarin and orange zests, the cornflour and the lemon and mandarin juice. Heat to 83-84°C. When the mixture reaches 60°C, whisk in the butter and pink peppercorns, then blend for 10 minutes with a hand blender. The crushed peppercorns will pleasantly flavour the cream without being overpowering.

Pour the cream into a gratin dish. Press clingfilm over the surface of the cream, then set aside in the fridge until next day.

Next day, make the macaron shells. Sift together the icing sugar and ground almonds. Stir the food colouring into the first portion of fresh egg whites. Pour them over the mixture of icing sugar and ground almonds but do not stir.

215g 'La Viette' butter (sweet butter from Charentes) at room temperature

5 pink peppercorns

+

120g 'La Viette' butter at room temperature

300g ground almonds

300g icing sugar

110g 'liquefied' egg whites (see page 11)

7g approx. lemon yellow food colouring

1g approx. carmine red food colouring

1g approx. strawberry red food colouring

+

300g caster sugar

75g mineral water

110g 'liquefied' egg whites (see page 11)

Bring the water and sugar to boil at 118°C. When the syrup reaches 115°C, simultaneously start whisking the second portion of liquefied egg whites to soft peaks.

When the sugar reaches 118°C, pour it over the egg whites. Whisk and allow the meringue to cool down to 50°C, then fold it into the almond-sugar mixture. Spoon the batter into a piping bag fitted with a plain nozzle. Pipe rounds of batter about 3.5 cm in diameter, spacing them 2 cm apart on baking trays lined with baking parchment. Rap the trays on the work surface covered with a kitchen cloth. Leave the shells to stand for about 30 minutes until they form a skin.

Preheat the fan oven to 180°C then put the trays in the oven. Bake for 12 minutes quickly opening and shutting the oven door twice during cooking time. Out of the oven, slide the shells on to the work surface.

For the mousseline cream of mandarin orange with pink peppercorns. Beat the butter for 5 minutes in the electric mixer fitted with the paddle attachment. Swap the paddle for a whisk. Add the mandarin orange cream you prepared the day before a third at a time. Whisk to obtain a smooth cream. Spoon the cream immediately into a piping bag with a plain nozzle.

Pipe a dot of cream on to half the macaron shells. Gently press a square of mandarin compote into the centre. Pipe a generous mound of cream on the shells and top with the remaining shells.

Store the macarons in the fridge for 24 hours then bring them back out 2 hours before serving.

A MADE-TO-MEASURE RECIPE FOR THE LAUNCH OF A NEW PRODUCT BY OCCITANE. OLIVIER BAUSSAN, THE BRAND'S FOUNDER, WANTED ME TO ADAPT COMPONENTS OF MANDARIN ORANGES AND PINK PEPPERCORNS, WHICH HE USED IN HIS PRODUCTS, TO CREATE A MACARON. IT GAVE ME THE CHANCE TO REDISCOVER A FRAGRANCE THAT I HADN'T MUCH LIKED IN COOKING. USUALLY, THE WHOLE BERRY IS USED IN VERY ORDINARY DISHES SO THAT YOU DON'T APPRECIATE THE SUBTLE, DELICATE FLAVOUR YOU WILL FIND IN THIS MACARON WHERE IT IS PAIRED WITH MANDARIN ORANGE.

ORANGE FLOWER, GINGER AND ROSE MACARON

Makes about 72 macarons
(or about 144 shells)

PREPARATION TIME:

about 1 hour

COOKING TIME:

about 25 minutes

STANDING TIME:

30 minutes

REFRIGERATION:

2 hours + 24 hours

FOR THE MACARON SHELLS

300g ground almonds

300g icing sugar

110g 'liquefied' egg whites
(see page 11)

1g approx. lemon yellow
food colouring

1g approx. strawberry red
food colouring

+

300g caster sugar

75g mineral water

110g 'liquefied' egg whites
(see page 11)

FOR THE ROSE AND
ORANGE FLOWER GANACHE

265g liquid crème fraîche or
whipping cream (35%
fat)

335g Valrhona Ivoire
couverture or white
chocolate

20g orange flower water

2g rose essence

20g rose syrup

15g candied orange peel

15g ginger preserved in
sugar

A MADE-TO-MEASURE MACARON FOR A CLIENT WHO WANTED TO BE PUT IN MIND OF THE AROMAS AND FLAVOURS OF HIS HOMELAND.

Sift together the icing sugar and ground almonds. Stir the food colouring into the first portion of liquefied egg whites. Pour them over the mixture of icing sugar and ground almonds but do not stir.

Bring the water and sugar to the boil at 118°C. When the syrup reaches 115°C, simultaneously start whisking the second portion of liquefied egg whites to soft peaks. When the sugar reaches 118°C, pour it over the egg whites. Whisk and allow the meringue to cool down to 50°C, then fold it into the almond-sugar mixture. Spoon the batter into a piping bag fitted with a plain nozzle.

Pipe rounds of batter about 3.5 cm in diameter, spacing them 2 cm apart on baking trays lined with baking parchment. Rap the trays on the work surface covered with a kitchen cloth. Leave the shells to stand for about 30 minutes until they form a skin.

Preheat the fan oven to 180°C then put the trays in the oven. Bake for 12 minutes quickly opening and shutting the oven door twice during cooking time. Out of the oven, slide the shells on to the work surface.

For the rose and orange flower ganache. Rinse the pieces of ginger and candied orange peel in warm water. Pat dry and chop them finely.

Chop up the chocolate and melt it in a bowl over a pan of barely simmering water. Bring the cream to the boil. Pour it over the melted chocolate a third at a time. Add the orange flower water, the rose essence and the rose syrup. Stir, then add the chopped ginger and orange peel. Stir everything together. Pour the mixture into a gratin dish. Press clingfilm over the surface of the ganache and set aside in the fridge for the ganache to thicken.

You can regulate the number of drops required, according to the strength of the rose essence and syrup and the orange flower water.

Spoon the ganache into a piping bag fitted with a plain nozzle. Pipe a generous mound of ganache on to half the shells and top with the remaining shells.

Store the macarons in the fridge for 24 hours then bring them back out 2 hours before serving.

MAISON DES TROIS THÉS MACARON

Gan Xiang tea ganache

A MADE-TO-MEASURE MACARON FOR MADAME TSENG, THE OWNER OF MAISON DES TROIS THÉS ON THE RUE SAINT MÉDARD IN PARIS. A VISIT TO HER SHOP IS A MAGICAL EXPERIENCE. A HEADY MIX OF AROMAS, SENSATIONS AND FLAVOURS WILL TRANSPORT YOU TO ANOTHER WORLD. AND MEETING MADAME TSENG IS AN EVENT YOU WILL NEVER FORGET: SHE IS A FOUNT OF WISDOM ON THE SUBJECT OF TEA AND HER BREADTH OF KNOWLEDGE IS TRULY IMPRESSIVE. GAN XIANG WAS HER CHOICE; ALL I DID WAS HUMBLY STRIVE TO DO IT JUSTICE.

Makes about 72 macarons
(or about 144 shells)

PREPARATION TIME:

about 1 hour

COOKING TIME:

about 25 minutes

STANDING TIME:

30 minutes

REFRIGERATION:

2 hours + 24 hours

FOR THE MACARON SHELLS

300g ground almonds

300g icing sugar

110g 'liquefied' egg whites
(see page 11)

2 Mexican vanilla pods

1 heaped teaspoon Gan
Xiang leaf tea (oolong)

+

300g caster sugar

75g mineral water

110g 'liquefied' egg whites
(see page 11)

FOR THE GAN XIANG TEA
GANACHE

330g liquid crème fraîche or
whipping cream (35%
fat)

30g Gan Xiang tea (oolong)

330g Valrhona Ivoire
couverture or white
chocolate

TO FINISH

Gan Xiang tea leaves
(oolong)

Sift together the icing sugar and ground almonds. Roughly chop the tea leaves. Split the vanilla pod in two and scrape out the seeds with the blade of a knife then add them to the mixture of icing sugar and ground almonds with the chopped tea. Pour the first portion of liquefied egg whites over the mixture of icing sugar and ground almonds but do not stir.

Bring the water and sugar to the boil at 118°C. When the syrup reaches 115°C, simultaneously start whisking the second portion of liquefied egg whites to soft peaks. When the sugar reaches 118°C, pour it over the egg whites. Whisk and allow the meringue to cool to 50°C, then fold it into the almond-sugar mixture. Spoon the batter into a piping bag fitted with a plain nozzle.

Pipe rounds of batter about 3.5 cm in diameter, spacing them 2 cm apart on baking trays lined with baking parchment. Rap the trays on the work surface covered with a kitchen cloth. Sprinkle the shells with 3 or 4 pieces of the chopped tea leaves. Leave the shells to stand for about 30 minutes until they form a skin.

Preheat the fan oven to 180°C then put the trays into the oven. Bake for 12 minutes quickly opening and shutting the oven door twice during cooking time. Out of the oven, slide the shells on to the work surface.

For the tea ganache. Put the tea in a sieve, pour 150g boiling water over the tea. Drain immediately, squeezing the water out of the leaves. Bring the cream to the boil. Take it off the heat and add the tea leaves. Cover with a lid and leave to infuse for five minutes then strain the cream.

Chop up the chocolate and melt it in a bowl over a pan of barely simmering water. Pour the cream over the melted chocolate a third at a time. Stir to obtain a smooth ganache. Pour the mixture into a gratin dish. Press clingfilm over the surface of the ganache and set aside in the fridge for the ganache to thicken.

Spoon the ganache into a piping bag fitted with a plain nozzle. Pipe a generous mound of ganache on to half the shells and top with the remaining shells.

Store the macarons in the fridge for 24 hours then bring them back out 2 hours before serving.

EXCEPTIONS

'INNOVATIONS AND INTERPRETATIONS BASED ON EXCEPTIONAL INGREDIENTS.'

MACARON OF 25-YEAR-OLD 'ACETO BALSAMICO DI MODENA'

Makes about 72 macarons
(or about 144 shells)

PREPARATION TIME:

about 1 hour

COOKING TIME:

about 25 minutes

STANDING TIME:

30 minutes

REFRIGERATION:

24 hours

FOR THE MACARON
SHELLS

300g ground almonds

300g icing sugar

60g cacao pâte or dark
chocolate, 100% cocoa
solids

110g 'liquefied' egg whites
(see page 11)

5g egg yellow food
colouring

+

300g caster sugar

75g mineral water

110g 'liquefied' egg whites
(see page 11)

The critical ingredient is balsamic vinegar sold in a wax-sealed bottle of 100ml and described in Italian as 'Aceto Balsamico Tradizionale di Modena'. It needs to have aged for 12 to 25 years. Other basic balsamic vinegars are not suitable for this delicate recipe.

Sift together the icing sugar and ground almonds. Chop up the cacao pâte and melt it at 50°C in a bowl over a pan of barely simmering water. Stir the food colouring into the first portion of liquefied egg whites. Pour them over the mixture of icing sugar and ground almonds but do not stir.

Bring the water and sugar to the boil at 118°C. When the syrup reaches 115°C, simultaneously start whisking the second portion of liquefied egg whites to soft peaks. When the sugar reaches 118°C, pour it over the egg whites. Whisk and allow the meringue to cool down to 50°C, then fold it into the almond-sugar mixture. Spoon the batter into a piping bag with a plain nozzle.

Pipe rounds of batter about 3.5 cm in diameter, spacing them 2 cm apart on baking trays lined with baking parchment. Rap the trays on the work surface covered with a kitchen cloth. Leave to stand for at least 30 minutes until a skin forms on the shells.

Preheat the fan oven to 180°C then put the trays in the oven. Bake for 12 minutes quickly opening and shutting the oven door twice during cooking time. Out of the oven, slide the shells on to the work surface.

For the ganache of traditional balsamic vinegar from Modena. Chop up the chocolate and melt it in a bowl over a pan of barely simmering water. (Cont.)

I WAS HAVING A TRADITIONAL SUNDAY EVENING DINNER WITH MY FRIEND THE ONCOLOGIST, DAVID KHAYAT, A COLLECTOR OF LUXURY BALSAMIC VINEGARS, WHEN I FIRST THOUGHT OF MAKING A MACARON BASED ON AN EXCEPTIONAL VINEGAR. WE HAD JUST BEEN SAMPLING A FEW, INCLUDING SOME THAT WERE OVER A HUNDRED YEARS OLD. I WAS TREMENDOUSLY EXCITED BY THE DISCOVERY OF FLAVOURS I HAD NEVER ENCOUNTERED BEFORE.

FOR THE GANACHE OF
'ACETO BALSAMICO DI
MODENA'

200g liquid crème fraîche
or whipping cream
(35% fat)

370g Valrhona Ivoire
couverture or white
chocolate

80g 25-year-old balsamic
vinegar from Modena

Bring the cream to the boil. Pour it over the chopped chocolate. Add the balsamic vinegar and blend for 2 minutes with a hand blender.

Pour the ganache into a gratin dish. Press clingfilm over the surface of the ganache and set aside in the fridge for the ganache to thicken.

Spoon the ganache into a piping bag with a plain nozzle. Pipe a generous mound of the ganache on to half the shells, then top with the remaining shells.

Store the macarons for 24 hours in the fridge. Bring them back out 2 hours before serving.

'ACETO BALSAMICO TRADIZIONALE DI MODENA' IS UNIQUE IN THE WORLD OF VINEGAR SEASONINGS. UNLIKE ALCOHOL-BASED VINEGAR, 'ACETO BALSAMICO' IS MADE FROM PURE GRAPE JUICE. THE 'MUST', A REDUCED JUICE OF LOCAL GRAPES THAT HAVE BEEN GROWN FOR CENTURIES ON THE SLOPES AROUND MODENA, IS COOKED IN AN OPEN VESSEL OVER AN OPEN FIRE, THEN POURED INTO PRECIOUS WOODEN CASKS. A HIGHLY COMPLEX PROCESS OF FERMENTATION AND OXIDATION CONCENTRATES THE FLAVOUR, AND THE VINEGAR MATURES FROM 12 TO 25 YEARS, ACCORDING TO THE PRODUCERS AND THE YEAR. THE TRADITION IS PERPETUATED BY A CONSORTIUM OF PRODUCERS OF TRADITIONAL BALSAMIC VINEGAR FROM MODENA. 'ACETO BALSAMICO TRADIZIONALE DI MODENA' IS PROTECTED BY BOTH ITALIAN AND EUROPEAN LAW. ON THE ADVICE OF EXPERT TASTERS, IT ALSO BENEFITS FROM A SPECIFIC DESIGNATION TO INDICATE ITS AGE, AND VINEGAR THAT HAS MATURED FOR MORE THAN 25 YEARS BEARS THE INSCRIPTION 'EXTRA VECCHIO'.

WHITE TRUFFLE AND PIEDMONT HAZELNUT MACARON

Makes about 72 macarons (or about 144 shells)

PREPARATION TIME:

about 1 hour 20 minutes

COOKING TIME:

about 40 minutes

STANDING TIME:

30 minutes

REFRIGERATION:

2 hours + 24 hours

FOR THE MACARON SHELLS

300g ground almonds

300g icing sugar

110g 'liquefied' egg whites (see page 11)

15g titanium oxide powder diluted in warm mineral water

+

300g caster sugar

75g mineral water

110g 'liquefied' egg whites (see page 11)

Start by preparing the roasted hazelnuts. Preheat the oven to 170°C. Spread out the hazelnuts on a baking tray. Put them in the oven and roast for about 15 minutes.

Put the hot nuts in a wide-mesh sieve or colander. Roll them around to remove the skins. Put them into a plastic bag and use a rolling pin to crush them into biggish pieces.

For the macaron shells. Sift together the icing sugar and ground almonds. Dilute the titanium oxide powder in the warm mineral water then stir it into the first portion of liquefied egg whites. Pour them over the mixture of icing sugar and ground almonds but do not stir.

Bring the water and sugar to the boil at 118°C. When the syrup reaches 115°C, simultaneously start whisking the second portion of liquefied egg whites to soft peaks.

When the sugar reaches 118°C, pour it over the egg whites. Whisk and allow the meringue to cool down to 50°C, then fold it into the almond-sugar mixture. Spoon the batter into a piping bag with a plain nozzle.

Pipe rounds of batter about 3.5 cm in diameter, spacing them 2 cm apart on baking trays lined with baking parchment.

Rap the trays on the work surface covered with a kitchen cloth. Sprinkle the shells with edible silver glitter. Leave to stand for at least 30 minutes until a skin forms on the shells.

Preheat the fan oven to 180°C then put the trays in the oven. Bake for 12 minutes quickly opening and shutting the oven door twice during

THIS MACARON BRINGS TOGETHER TWO SPECIALITY PRODUCTS FROM PIEDMONT: ALBA WHITE TRUFFLE AND HAZELNUTS WHICH MAKE A WONDERFUL PAIRING. IT WAS FIRST PRODUCED FOR THE AUTUMN/WINTER 2002 'BLANC COUSU MAIN' ('HAND-STITCHED WHITE') PIERRE HERMÉ COLLECTION.

350g Valrhona Ivoire
couverture or white
chocolate

350g liquid crème
fraîche or whipping
cream (35% fat)

45g fresh Alba white
truffle

FOR THE ROASTED
HAZELNUTS

220g Piedmont
hazelnuts

TO FINISH

Edible silver glitter (see
page 205)

*Piedmont hazelnuts can be
difficult to find and the ones
sold commercially are often
poor quality when not actually
rancid. I suggest looking
further afield. If you are lucky
enough to find Piedmont
hazelnuts, you will recognise
them because they are bigger
than ordinary hazelnuts and
have a unique suave, sweetish
flavour.*

cooking time. Out of the oven, slide the shells on to the work surface.

For the white truffle ganache. Finely chop the 30g truffle. Chop up the chocolate and melt it in a bowl over a pan of barely simmering water. Bring the cream to the boil.

Pour the cream over the chocolate a third at a time and allow to cool before adding the chopped truffle and stirring.

Pour the ganache into a gratin dish. Press clingfilm over the surface of the ganache and set aside in the fridge for the ganache to thicken.

Spoon the ganache into a piping bag with a plain nozzle. Pipe a generous mound of the ganache on to half the shells. Gently press 3 or 4 pieces of hazelnut into the centre, then top with the remaining shells.

Store the macarons for 24 hours in the fridge. Bring them back out 2 hours before serving.

FOIE GRAS AND CHOCOLATE MACARON

Makes about 72 macarons
(or about 144 shells)

PREPARATION TIME:

about 1 hour 30 minutes

COOKING TIME:

about 55 minutes

STANDING TIME:

30 minutes

REFRIGERATION:

24 hours

FOR THE FOIE GRAS JELLY
SQUARES

100g water

A quarter chicken stock
cube or

100g home-made chicken
stock

200g semi-preserved fresh
duck foie gras

20g caster sugar

2 drops Tabasco sauce

2 grinds of Sarawak black
pepper

3g gelatine leaves

FOR THE MACARON SHELLS

300g ground almonds

300g icing sugar

110g 'liquefied' egg whites
(see page 11)

30g approx. strawberry red
food colouring

+

300g caster sugar

75g mineral water

110g 'liquefied' egg whites
(see page 11)

Start by preparing the squares of foie gras jelly. Soak the gelatine for 15 minutes in cold water to soften. Force the foie gras through a fine-mesh sieve to obtain a fine purée. Bring the water to the boil with the crumbled chicken stock cube, the fois gras purée, Tabasco sauce, the sugar and the pepper (the boiling liquid will separate but don't worry, when you have processed it, it will be smooth).

Off the heat, blend with a hand blender to obtain a smooth mixture. Add the drained gelatine and blend for 1 minute, then pour into a gratin dish lined with clingfilm to a depth of 4 mm. Smooth the surface and set aside in the fridge to cool for 1 hour then transfer the dish to the freezer for 2 hours. Turn the slab out of the dish and cut it into 1.5 cm squares. Return the squares to the freezer.

For the macaron shells. Sift together the icing sugar with the ground almonds. Stir the food colouring into the first portion of liquefied egg whites. Pour them over the mixture of icing sugar and ground almonds but do not stir.

Bring the water and sugar to the boil at 118°C. When the syrup reaches 115°C, simultaneously start whisking the second portion of liquefied egg whites to soft peaks.

When the sugar reaches 118°C, pour it over the egg whites. Whisk and allow the meringue to cool down to 50°C, then fold it into the almond-sugar mixture. Spoon the batter into a piping bag with a plain nozzle.

Pipe rounds of batter about 3.5 cm in diameter, spacing them 2 cm apart on baking trays lined with baking parchment. Rap the trays on the work surface covered with a kitchen cloth. Sprinkle the shells with gold glitter or, at the end of cooking, with flakes of gold leaf. Leave to stand for at least 30 minutes until a skin forms on the shells.

Preheat the fan oven to 180°C then put the trays in the oven. Bake for 12 minutes quickly opening and shutting the oven door twice during cooking time. Out of the oven, slide the shells on to the work surface.

For the chocolate ganache. Chop up the chocolate and melt it in a bowl over a pan of barely simmering water. Bring the cream to the boil. Pour the cream over the melted chocolate a third at a time.

250g liquid crème fraîche or
    whipping cream (35% fat)

220g Valrhona Jivara
    couverture or milk
    chocolate, 40% cocoa
    solids

30g Valrhona Guanaja
    couverture, 70% cocoa
    solids

TO FINISH

Gold leaf

or

Edible gold glitter (see page
    205)

Pour the ganache into a gratin dish. Press clingfilm over the surface of the ganache and set aside in the fridge for the ganache to thicken.

Spoon the ganache into a piping bag with a plain nozzle. Pipe a dot of ganache on to half the shells. Gently press a square of jelly into the centre. Fill the shells generously with ganache, then top with the remaining shells.

Store the macarons for 24 hours in the fridge. Bring them back out 2 hours before serving.

A MACARON INSPIRED BY THE RECIPE FOR HOT, PAN-FRIED FOIE GRAS WITH COCOA NIBS BY MY FRIEND HÉLÈNE DARROZE. TO MAKE SURE THE CHOCOLATE DOESN'T OVERPOWER THE FOIE GRAS, I USE LESS BITTER CHOCOLATE AND MAKE A MILK CHOCOLATE GANACHE ENLIVENED WITH A HINT OF DARK CHOCOLATE.

OSETRA CAVIAR AND WALNUT BRANDY MACARON

Makes about 72
  macarons (or about
  144 shells)

PREPARATION TIME:

about 1 hour

COOKING TIME:

about 12 minutes

STANDING TIME:

30 minutes

REFRIGERATION:

4 hours

FOR THE WALNUT
AND CAVIAR JELLY

520g mineral water

190g walnut brandy
  (from Denoix)

17g gelatine leaves

200g Osetra caviar

Start by preparing the rounds of caviar and walnut liqueur jelly. Soak the gelatine for 15 minutes in cold water to soften. Drain and melt it in a bowl over a pan of barely simmering water or in the microwave. When the gelatine has melted, add the mineral water and walnut liqueur. Divide it, to a depth of 2 mm, among 36 flexible silicon mini-baking cases measuring about 4 cm in diameter. Allow the jelly to set in the fridge.

When the jelly has set, add 5g caviar to each mini-baking case. Top with 2 mm high dabs of the rest of the walnut liqueur jelly. Return the cases to the fridge for the jelly to set again until the last minute.

For the macaron shells. Sift together the icing sugar with the ground almonds then pour them over the first portion of liquefied egg whites but do not stir.

Bring the water and sugar to the boil at 118°C. When the syrup reaches 115°C, simultaneously start whisking the second portion of liquefied egg whites to soft peaks.

When the sugar reaches 118°C, pour it over the egg whites. Whisk and allow the meringue to cool down to 50°C, then fold it into the almond-sugar mixture. Spoon the batter into a piping bag with a plain nozzle.

Pipe rounds of batter about 3.5 cm in diameter, spacing them 2 cm apart on baking trays lined with baking parchment. Rap the trays on the

A SPECIAL MACARON, EXCEPTIONAL AND EPHEMERAL. IN 1989, FOR A DINNER WHERE CAVIAR TOOK PRIDE OF PLACE, I SET MYSELF THE CHALLENGE OF COMPOSING A DESSERT SERVED IN AN ICED GLASS: A WALNUT BRANDY SORBET TOPPED WITH A GENEROUS SPOONFUL OF OSETRA CAVIAR -- 10G. THE EXPERTS I CONSULTED PROCLAIMED THE CAVIAR TO HAVE A DELICATE WALNUT FLAVOUR. I WAS VERY EXCITED BY THE IDEA AND I USED WALNUT BRANDY FROM DENOIX -- YOU DON'T MAKE UP THAT KIND OF THING! I FOUND ITS FLAVOUR TO BE THE IDEAL PAIRING WITH THE CAVIAR.

FOR THE MACARON
SHELLS

150g ground almonds

150g icing sugar

55g 'liquefied' egg
   whites (see page 11)

+

150g caster sugar

38g mineral water

55g 'liquefied' egg
   whites (see page 11)

TO FINISH

Flakes of white gold
   leaf

or

Edible silver glitter (see
   page 205)

Osetra caviar is becoming
increasingly difficult to find,
and I often use Prunier's
caviar d'Aquitaine, or I buy it
from Alan Jones of Sturgeon
in Saint Sulpice Cameyrac,
whose outstanding caviar I
particularly appreciate.

work surface covered with a kitchen cloth. Sprinkle the shells with silver glitter or, at the end of the cooking time, with flakes of white gold leaf. Leave to stand for at least 30 minutes until a skin forms on the shells.

Preheat the fan oven to 180°C then put the trays in the oven. Bake for 12 minutes quickly opening and shutting the oven door twice during cooking time. Out of the oven, slide the shells on to the work surface. Put the mini-baking cases with the rounds of jelly in the freezer for 15 minutes to make it easier to turn them out of the moulds.

Using a small spatula, carefully take the jelly rounds out of the cases one by one.

Place them one at a time on half the shells. Top with the remaining shells. Store them in the fridge until serving. They need to be eaten the same day and no longer than 5 hours after they were made.

ROSEHIP, FIG AND FOIE GRAS MACARON

Makes about 72 macarons
(or about 144 shells)

PREPARATION TIME:

about 1 hour 30 minutes

COOKING TIME:

about 55 minutes

STANDING TIME:

30 minutes

REFRIGERATION:

24 hours

FOR THE FOIE GRAS JELLY
SQUARES

100g water

A quarter chicken stock
cube or

100g home-made chicken
stock

200g semi-preserved fresh
duck foie gras

20g caster sugar

2 drops Tabasco sauce

2 grinds of Sarawak black
pepper

3g gelatine leaves

FOR THE MACARON SHELLS

300g ground almonds

300g icing sugar

110g 'liquefied' egg whites
(see page 11)

15g titanium oxide powder
diluted in 10g warm
mineral water

+

300g caster sugar

75g mineral water

110g 'liquefied' egg whites
(see page 11)

Don't use standard dried figs, as their flavour is unsuitable for this recipe. Instead, choose partially rehydrated figs.

When I was a boy growing up in Alsace, my mother used to serve rosehip jam at breakfast and I'm sure that is why I'm so partial to the flavour. However, there are very few producers of rosehip purée, apart from Beyer in Mulhouse.

Start by preparing the squares of foie gras jelly. Soak the gelatine for 15 minutes in cold water to soften.

Force the foie gras through a fine-mesh sieve to obtain a fine purée. Bring the water to the boil with the crumbled stock cube, the fois gras purée, Tabasco sauce, the sugar and the pepper (the boiling liquid will separate but don't worry, when you have blended it, it will be smooth).

Off the heat, blend with a hand blender to obtain a smooth mixture. Add the drained gelatine and blend for 1 minute, then pour the purée into a gratin dish lined with clingfilm to a depth of 4 mm. Smooth the surface and set aside in the fridge to cool for 1 hour then transfer the dish to the freezer for 2 hours. Turn the slab out of the dish and cut it into 1.5 cm squares. Return the squares to the freezer.

For the macaron shells. Sift together the icing sugar and ground almonds. Dilute the titanium oxide powder in the warm water. Stir it into the first portion of liquefied egg whites. Pour them over the mixture of icing sugar and ground almonds but do not stir.

Bring the water and sugar to the boil at 118°C. When the syrup reaches 115°C, simultaneously start whisking the second portion of liquefied egg whites to soft peaks.

When the sugar reaches 118°C, pour it over the egg whites. Whisk and allow the meringue to cool down to 50°C, then fold it into the almond-sugar mixture. Spoon the batter into a piping bag with a plain nozzle.

Pipe rounds of batter about 3.5 cm in diameter, spacing them 2 cm apart on baking trays lined with baking parchment. Rap the trays on the work surface covered with a kitchen cloth. Sprinkle the shells with gold glitter or, at the end of cooking, with flakes of gold leaf. Leave to stand for at least 30 minutes until a skin forms on the shells.

Preheat the fan oven to 180°C then put the trays in the oven. Bake for 12 minutes quickly opening and shutting the oven door twice during cooking time.

250g rosehip purée
(see page 204)

330g Valrhona Ivoire
couverture or white
chocolate

90g soft figs (in
packets from the
dried-fruit aisle)

TO FINISH

Flakes of gold leaf

or

Edible gold glitter (see
page 205)

Out of the oven, slide the shells on to the work surface.

For the chocolate, rosehip and fig ganache. Chop up the chocolate and melt it in a bowl over a pan of barely simmering water. Heat the rosehip purée to 50°C. Pour it over the melted chocolate a third at a time. Add the figs. Blend for 2 minutes using a hand blender. Pour the ganache into a gratin dish. Press clingfilm over the surface of the ganache and set aside in the fridge for the ganache to thicken.

Spoon the ganache into a piping bag with a plain nozzle. Pipe a generous mound of ganache on to half the shells. Gently press a square of jelly into the centre, then top with the remaining shells.

Store the macarons for 24 hours in the fridge. Bring them back out 2 hours before serving.

USING FOIE GRAS IN MY CAKES CAME NATURALLY TO ME. ALTHOUGH IT IS ALWAYS SERVED AS AN ACCOMPANIMENT TO SWEET AND/OR SOUR DISHES, IN 1989, I TOOK THE INNOVATIVE STEP OF CREATING A CRÈME BRÛLÉE DESSERT WITH FOIE GRAS. I WAS KEEN TO TRY A FOIE GRAS MACARON BUT HAD NOT FOUND A WAY OF REDUCING THE GREASY TEXTURE WITHOUT SUP-PRESSING THE FLAVOUR. I FINALLY OVERCAME THAT HURDLE WITH A JELLY. IN COMBINATION WITH THE SLIGHT TARTNESS OF SOFT FIGS AND THE TANGINESS OF ROSEHIP, I CONSIDER IT A PER-FECT MARRIAGE OF FLAVOURS.

BLACK TRUFFLE MACARON

I USED THESE BLACK TRUFFLES BY THE LEGENDARY COMPANY PEBEYRE IN CAHORS TO RECREATE AN EMOTIONAL CULINARY MOMENT: THE MEMORY OF A BOILED EGG PREPARED FOR ME BY KEN HOM, THE WORLD-FAMOUS CHINESE CHEF. HE SERVED IT WITH PÉRIGORD BLACK TRUFFLE, MELTED BUTTER AND BREAD SOLDIERS.

Makes about 72 macarons
(or about 144 shells)

PREPARATION TIME:

about 1 hour

COOKING TIME:

about 25 minutes

STANDING TIME:

30 minutes

REFRIGERATION:

2 hours + 24 hours

FOR THE MACARON
SHELLS

300g ground almonds

300g icing sugar

110g 'liquefied' egg
whites (see page 11)

15g approx. black food
colouring (see advice
below)

+

300g caster sugar

75g mineral water

110g 'liquefied' egg
whites (see page 11)

FOR THE BLACK TRUFFLE
GANACHE

400g liquid crème fraîche
or whipping cream
(35% fat)

80g whole fresh *Tuber
Melanosporum* black
truffles (or Pebeyre
preserved whole black
truffles)

500g Valrhona Ivoire
couverture or white
chocolate

Instead of the black shells which need black food colouring, you can prepare white macaron shells using 15g titanium oxide diluted in 10g warm mineral water and add little pieces of black truffles. I suggest you avoid the black truffle flavouring which would spoil irrevocably the exceptional aroma of *Tuber Melanosporum* truffle from the Périgord or the Luberon.

Sift together the icing sugar and ground almonds. Stir the food colouring into the first portion of liquefied egg whites. Pour them over the mixture of icing sugar and ground almonds but do not stir.

Bring the water and sugar to the boil at 118°C. When the syrup reaches 115°C, simultaneously start whisking the second portion of liquefied egg whites to soft peaks.

When the sugar reaches 118°C, pour it over the egg whites. Whisk and allow the meringue to cool down to 50°C, then fold it into the almond-sugar mixture. Spoon the batter into a piping bag with a plain nozzle.

Pipe rounds of batter about 3.5 cm in diameter, spacing them 2 cm apart on baking trays lined with baking parchment. Rap the trays on the work surface covered with a kitchen cloth. Leave to stand for at least 30 minutes until a skin forms on the shells.

Preheat the fan oven to 180°C then put the trays in the oven. Bake for 12 minutes quickly opening and shutting the oven door twice during cooking time. Out of the oven, slide the shells on to the work surface.

For the black truffle ganache. Chop up the chocolate and melt it in a bowl over a pan of barely simmering water.

Bring the cream to the boil. Finely chop the truffles. Blend the chopped truffle for 2 minutes with the cream in an electric mixer or using a hand blender. Pour the cream over the melted chocolate a third at a time. Stir to obtain a smooth ganache. Pour the ganache into a gratin dish. Press clingfilm over the surface of the ganache and set aside in the fridge for the ganache to thicken.

Spoon the ganache into a piping bag with a plain nozzle. Pipe a generous mound of the ganache on to half the shells, then top with the remaining shells.

Store the macarons for 24 hours in the fridge. Bring them back out 2 hours before serving.

DÉLICIEUX MACARON
Grapefruit and wasabi

Makes about 72
macarons (or about
144 shells)

PREPARATION TIME:

the day before, 15
minutes; next day,
about 1 hour

COOKING TIME:

about 1 hour 50
minutes

STANDING TIME:

30 minutes

REFRIGERATION:

2 hours + 24 hours

FOR THE CANDIED
GRAPEFRUIT

2 untreated grapefruit

1 litre water

500g caster sugar

1 star anise

10g Sarawak black
peppercorns

1 vanilla pod

4 tablespoons lemon
juice

The day before, wash and dry the grapefruits. Cut off both ends. Using a knife, cut thick segments from top to bottom and trim away the peel and a good centimetre of flesh.

Immerse the zests obtained in a pan of boiling water. Bring the water back to the boil and cook for 2 minutes then drain. Refresh in cold water. Repeat this step twice more. Drain the zests.

Grind the peppercorns. Put them into a saucepan with the water, sugar and lemon juice, the star anise and the split vanilla pod with the seeds scraped out. Bring to the boil over a low heat. Add the grapefruit segments. Put a lid on the pan so that it three-quarters covers it and simmer very gently for 1 hour 30 minutes.

Put the grapefruit segments and syrup in a bowl. Allow to cool. Cover with clingfilm and set aside in the fridge until next day.

For the ground pistachios to finish. Preheat the oven to 90°C. Put the pistachios into the oven on a baking tray. Allow to dry for about 3 hours. Out of the oven, allow them to cool before grinding them in the food processor. Sift to a fine powder.

Next day, in a sieve over a bowl, drain the zests for an hour. Cut the zests into 4 mm cubes.

For the macaron shells. Sift together the icing sugar and ground almonds. Dilute the titanium oxide powder in the warm mineral water then stir it into the first portion of liquefied egg whites. Pour them into the mixture of icing sugar and ground almonds but do not stir.

Bring the water and sugar to the boil at 118°C. When the syrup reaches

I WANTED TO PLAY UP THE SHARP BUT FLEETING FLAVOUR OF WASABI AND THE BITTER, TANGY TASTE OF GRAPEFRUIT. MY FIRST IDEA IN 1998 WAS FOR A SORBET, BUT I ABANDONED IT BECAUSE, BACK THEN, I COULD NOT GET HOLD OF THE RHIZOME IN PARIS. WHEN I FINALLY DID, IN 2007, I CREATED A DESSERT AND THIS MACARON.

300g ground almonds

300g icing sugar

110g 'liquefied' egg
whites (see page 11)

15g titanium oxide
powder diluted in
10g warm mineral
water

+

300g caster sugar

75g mineral water

110g 'liquefied' egg
whites (see page 11)

FOR THE WASABI
GANACHE

40g yuzu juice or lime
juice

300g liquid crème
fraîche or whipping
cream (35% fat)

375g Valrhona Ivoire
couverture or white
chocolate

20g grated fresh
wasabi, available in
Japanese shops, or
wasabi paste sold in
tubes

TO FINISH

150g shelled unsalted
pistachios

In Japan, fresh wasabi is grated with a special grater made of dried sharkskin or a small-toothed ceramic grater. If you don't have one of these, use a Microplane grater.

Wasabi is a hardy plant that is grown for its root. It is a kind of Japanese horseradish, pale in colour and with an extremely powerful flavour but not as strong as western horseradish. It belongs to the same botanical family as horseradish and mustard. Wasabi is grown in Japan, China, Thailand and the United States, among other countries.

115°C, simultaneously start whisking the second portion of liquefied egg whites to soft peaks. When the sugar reaches 118°C, pour it over the egg whites. Whisk and allow the meringue to cool down to 50°C, then fold it into the almond-sugar mixture. Spoon the batter into a piping bag with a plain nozzle.

Pipe rounds of batter about 3.5 cm in diameter, spacing them 2 cm apart on baking trays lined with baking parchment. Rap the trays on the work surface covered with a kitchen cloth. Sprinkle with the ground pistachio. Leave to stand for at least 30 minutes until a skin forms on the shells.

Preheat the fan oven to 180°C then put the trays in the oven. Bake for 12 minutes quickly opening and shutting the oven door twice during cooking time. Out of the oven, slide the shells on to the work surface.

For the wasabi ganache. Chop up the chocolate and melt it in a bowl over a pan of barely simmering water. Heat the yuzu juice to 40°C. Bring the cream to the boil.

Peel the wasabi. Grate it using a wasabi grater if possible. Weigh out 20g. Pour the hot cream over the chocolate half at a time then add the yuzu juice a little at a time, then the grated fresh wasabi. Transfer the ganache to a gratin dish. Press clingfilm over the surface of the ganache and set aside in the fridge for the ganache to thicken.

Pour the ganache into a piping bag with a plain nozzle. Pipe a generous mound of the ganache on to half the shells. Gently press 2 or 3 cubes of candied grapefruit into the ganache then top with the remaining shells.

Store in the fridge for 24 hours and bring back out 2 hours before serving.

USEFUL ADDRESSES

*List of suppliers of the products recommended by Pierre Hermé
(with, where available, alternative suppliers outside France)*

Pierre Hermé's macarons are available from Selfridges in London and

Pierre Hermé
13 Lowndes Street
London SW1X 9EX
Tel: 020 7245 0317
www.pierreherme.com

ALL THE CHOCOLATE COUVERTURES (DARK, IVOIRE, MILK, CACAO PÂTE, COCOA NIBS)

Valrhona
From delicatessens and fine food stores and
www.valrhona.com

CHUAO CHOCOLATE

The Chuao cocoa bean, named after the plantation and defined geographical area in which it is grown, is considered to produce some of the finest chocolate in the world.

Top producers are Amedei and Domori. Available from Harvey Nichols, Harrods, Fortnum and Mason and Selfridges and online from
www.chocolatetradingco.com
www.seventypercent.com

Or Amedei can be bought on line from its UK distributors:

King's Fine Foods Limited
2 Mill Farm Business Park
Millfield Road
Hanworth
Middlesex TW4 5PY
Tel: 020 8894 1111
www.kingsfinefood.co.uk

GIANDUJA (WRAPPED IN GOLD PAPER)

This is a traditional Italian confection made of hazelnut praline and chocolate.

Available from delicatessens, Italian food shops and chocolatiers and online from
www.leonidasbelgianchocolates.co.uk

MARRONS GLACÉS, CHESTNUT PASTE, CHESTNUT PURÉE AND CHESTNUT CREAM

Available from most quality food shops

Corsiglia Facor
455, chemin de la Vallée
13400 Aubagne
Tel. : 04 42 36 99 99
www.corsigliafacor.com

PURE PISTACHIO PASTE, FLAVOURED AND COLOURED PISTACHIO PASTE, HAZELNUT PASTE

Bronte Crema di Pistacchio from Sicily is available from

Melbury & Appleton
271 Muswell Hill Broadway
London N10
Tel: 020 8442 0558
www.melburyandappleton.co.uk

Other products from
www.patiwizz.com
www.sevarôme.com

ROSE ESSENCE

Rose essence is a more concentrated form of rose flavouring than rose water.

Available from some Middle Eastern and Indian food shops

ROSE SYRUP (SHAH BRAND)

Shah & Cie

33 rue Notre-Dame-de-Lorette
75009 Paris
Tel: 01 42 85 55 16

Monin brand is available in Polish, Indian and Iranian shops

www.thedrinksshop.com

ROSEHIP PURÉE

Available from some Middle Eastern food shops
Buy online from

www.efoodies.co.uk
www.lepicerie.com

VANILLA FROM TAHITI, MADAGASCAR, MEXICO

www.vanillamart.co.uk
www.vanillabazaar.com

GRIOTTINES® CHERRIES (MORELLO CHERRIES MACERATED IN KIRSCH)

www.griottines.co.uk

ORANGE MARMALADE

Christine Ferber is a fourth-generation pastry chef and jam maker in Alsace

Pâtisserie Christine Ferber

18 rue des Trois-Épis
68230 Niedermorschwihr
Tel: 03 89 27 05 69

SPICES: SAFFRON, CEYLON CINNAMON, SARAWAK PEPPER, STAR ANISE, PINK PEPPERCORNS

The Spice Shop

1 Blenheim Crescent
London W11 2EE
Tel: 020 7221 4448
www.thespiceshop.co.uk

ESPELETTE CHILLI PEPPER

www.pimentdespellete.com

Purchase online from

www.oliversandco.com
www.thegoodfoodnetwork.co.uk

YUZU PURÉE, GREEN TEA AND ALL JAPANESE PRODUCTS

Japanese food shops and online from

www.japanesekitchen.co.uk
www.teapigs.co.uk

MATCHA GREEN TEA

This is finely-milled green tea
Available from Oriental grocers or online from

www.jingtea.com
www.japanesekitchen.co.uk

XIANG GAN TEA

This is a Chinese Oolong tea which Pierre Hermé sources from Maison des Trois Thés in Paris.

www.troisthés.com

A Tie Guan Yin tea is available from

www.jingtea.com

TEN-YEAR-OLD 'OLD BROWN JM AGRICOLE RUM'

produced in Martinique and available from

Corks of Cotham

54 Cotham Hill,
Cotham,
Bristol,
BS6 6JX
Tel: 0117 973 1620
www.corksof.com

Gerry's Wines and Spirits

74 Old Compton Street
London W1
Tel: 020 7734 4215
www.gerrys.uk.com

and online from

www.thedrinkshop.com

EAU DE VIE ABRICOTINE DU VALAIS (MORAND)

Georges Barbier of London Ltd

267 Lee High Road
London SE12 8RU
Tel: 020 8852 5801

And online from

www.morand.ch

Also always worth trying Gerry's Wine and Spirits (see under TEN-YEAR-OLD 'OLD BROWN JM AGRICOLE RUM') who are able to source most unusual drinks

WALNUT BRANDY

Denoix Maitre Liquoriste

9, boulevard du Maréchal Lyautey
BP236
19108 Brive-la-Gaillarde
Tel: 05 55 74 34 27
www.denoix.fr

and also from

www.cherry-rocher.fr

Also Gerry's Wine and Spirits (see under TEN-YEAR OLD 'OLD BROWN JM AGRICOLE RUM')

FOOD COLOURING (NATURAL)

Pierre Hermé uses Sevarôme

www.sevarôme.fr

but try the following outside France

The Spice Shop

1 Blenheim Crescent
London W11 2EE
Tel: 020 7221 4448
http://www.thespiceshop.co.uk

also available online from

www.chocolatecraftcolors.com

EDIBLE SPARKLES (FOR DECORATING THE MACARONS)

Pierre Hermé uses PCB Création,

www.pcb-creation.fr

But there are many online suppliers of edible glitters such as

www.cakecraftshop.co.uk
www.cakescookiesandcraftsshop.co.uk
www.fairygoodies.co.uk

OLIVE OIL

Pierre Hermé uses the oils from producers Pierre Grimat of Gaïa Bio, Bernard Cavallo of Moulin du Grimaudet, Alain Monnier of Mas de L'Ange and Laurent Badré of Domaine Mas Sénéguier but these will be difficult to find outside France

PARMESAN

Parmigiano Reggiano DOP Vacche Rosse (Red Cow) Made from the ancient Reggiana breed of cow, aged for 30 months.

Pierre Hermé uses this Parmesan which is exclusive to

Épicerie Da Rosa

62 rue de Seine 75006 Paris
Tel: 09 79 07 52 22
www.restaurant-da-rosa.com

CAVIAR D'AQUITAINE

www.efoodies.co.uk

FRESH AND PRESEVED BLACK TRUFFLES/ WHITE TRUFFLES

Most good Italian delicatessens will stock preserved truffles

Wild Harvest

Units B61-64
New Covent Garden Market
London
SW8 5HH
Tel: 020 7498 5397 (24 hours)
www.wildharvestuk.com

ACKNOWLEDGEMENTS

Pierre Hermé

My thanks to my friend and associate, Charles Znaty, without whom the Pierre Hermé Macaron would never have seen the light of day or become what it has throughout the world. I must also thank Coco Jobard for her patience and help with the text, as well as Bernhard Winkelmann for magnifying the macaron with his beautiful photography, and Mickael Marsollier and Anna Plagens for working so devotedly with me on this book.

Coco Jobard

I am immensely grateful to Pierre Hermé for his faith in me.

My thanks for her kindness and precious help to Anna Plagens, assistant knowledge coordinator at Pierre Hermé, who so skilfully made all the macarons.

Thanks to Colette Petremant, executive director at Pierre Hermé and Mickael Marsollier, knowledge coordinator at Pierre Hermé, for their valuable advice.

Thanks to Julien de Sousa for his support and patience during my two-day placement to learn how to make macarons in the training workshop at the Haute Pâtisserie Pierre Hermé at the Ecole Ferrandi.

Warmest thanks to everyone who kindly lent items and utensils for the photos.

Christine
Boutique Toquades
70, boulevard Malesherbes
75008 Paris
Tél. : 01 45 61 03 13.
www.toquades.fr
where you will find all the necessary utensils to make the macarons

Ariane Lackenbacher
Marie Papier
26, rue Vavin
75006 Paris
www.mariepapier.fr

Dominique Boulanger
Trait
35, rue de Jussieu
75005 Paris
www.trait.fr

Caroline Lheritier
Zwilling
12, boulevard de la Madeleine
75009 Paris
www.zwilling.com

to Barbara, my wife
to Sarah

This English language edition published in 2011 by
Grub Street
4 Rainham Close
London
SW11 6SS
Email: food@grubstreet.co.uk
Web: www.grubstreet.co.uk

Reprinted 2011 (twice), 2012 (three times), 2013 (twice), 2014

Copyright this English language edition © Grub Street 2011
Translation by Tamsin Black
Copyright original French edition © Agnès Viénot Éditions, 2008
Originally published in France as *Macaron* by Agnès Viénot Éditions, Paris
A CIP catalogue record for this book is available from the British Library

ISBN 978-1-908117-23-6

All rights reserved. No part of this book may be reproduced or transmitted in any form or by any
means, electronic or mechanical, including photocopying, recording or any information storage and
retrieval system, without permission in writing from the publisher.

Printed and bound in Slovenia